IS HE DEAD?

IS HE DEAD?

A COMEDY IN THREE ACTS

mark twain

Edited with Foreword, Afterword, and Notes by
SHELLEY FISHER FISHKIN

Text Established by
THE MARK TWAIN PROJECT, THE BANCROFT LIBRARY

Illustrations by
BARRY MOSER

UNIVERSITY OF CALIFORNIA PRESS
Berkeley   Los Angeles   London

*Frontispiece: Portrait of Mark Twain, painted in Vienna in
1898 by Ignace Spiridon. Twain was friends with the painter.
Courtesy Mark Twain Papers, The Bancroft Library.*

University of California Press

Berkeley and Los Angeles, California

University of California Press, Ltd.

London, England

© 2003 by the Regents of the University of California.The
text of *Is He Dead?* by Mark Twain is © 2002, 2003 by Richard A.
Watson and J. P. Morgan Chase Manhattan Bank as Trustees of the
Mark Twain Foundation, which reserves all reproduction or
dramatization rights in every medium. The editorial foreword,
afterword, and notes are © 2003 by Shelley Fisher Fishkin.
Illustrations by Barry Moser on cover and pp. 5, 49, and
101 are © 2003 by Barry Moser.

Library of Congress Cataloging-in-Publication Data

Twain, Mark, 1835–1910.
Is he dead? : a comedy in three acts / Mark Twain ; edited with
foreword, afterword, and notes by Shelley Fisher Fishkin ;
text established by the Mark Twain Project, the Bancroft
Library ; illustrations by Barry Moser.
p. cm.—(Jumping frogs ; 1)
Includes bibliographical references.
ISBN: 0-520-23979-2 (cloth : alk. paper)
1. Artists—Drama. 2. Barbizon (France)—Drama.
3. Death—Drama. I. Fishkin, Shelley Fisher. II. Title.

PS1322.17 2003
812'.4—dc21 2003050703

Manufactured in the United States of America
13 12 11 10 09 08 07 06 05 04
10 9 8 7 6 5 4 3 2 1

The paper used in this publication meets the
minimum requirements of ANSI/NISO Z39.48–
1992(R 1997) *(Permanence of Paper).*

contents

Facing pages from Mark Twain's notebook in which he mentions *Is He Dead?* twice.
On the left-hand page, he writes "Is He Dead? Millet the painter" and jots down notes
for a possible denouement that he did not use. On the right-hand page, he writes
"Jan. 14, 1898. Began to write comedy 'Is he Dead?' (François Millet.)"
Courtesy Mark Twain Papers, The Bancroft Library.

foreword

Mark Twain wrote this high-spirited romp of a play in the winter of 1898, as he emerged from one of the deepest depressions of his life. It is printed here for the first time.

The sudden death of Twain's eldest daughter, Susy, at age twenty-four in August of 1896 had left a gaping hole in his heart. He tried to ease the pain through work, completing his travel book *Following the Equator* and starting several other projects.[1] But little that he wrote during this time suited him— "because of the deadness which invaded me when Susy died."[2] Grief mingled with despair: Twain had declared bankruptcy several years earlier, and there was still no sign that he would ever get out of debt.[3] "I have lost three entire months, now," he wrote in early November 1897. "In that time I have begun twenty magazine articles and books—and flung every one of them aside in turn." Since last August, Twain wrote, "I have finished not *one single thing.*"[4]

Twain penned these lines from Vienna, then Europe's third largest city, where he had moved his family in the fall of 1897 to indulge his twenty-three-year-old daughter Clara's musical ambitions—specifically, her desire to study piano with Theodor Leschetizky, the renowned Viennese instructor. The family's arrival in Vienna without hotel reservations on a dreary day at the end of September had been inauspicious. "No one could have believed, as we turned our lights out in our dingy rooms that night, that Vienna would ever come to seem a pleasant place," Clara recalled. The heartache that the first anniversary of Susy's death in August had brought to the surface, the continuing financial pressure, the challenge of getting his family settled in a foreign city, and, to make matters worse, an episode of gout, all added to the gloom. In early December, news arrived that Twain's brother Orion had passed away, and shortly thereafter Twain learned that his friend George

Griffin, the family's former butler in Hartford, Connecticut, had also passed away. Feeling ground down by debt and depressed by grief, Twain wrote his publisher, "It has been reported that I am writing books—for publication; I am not doing anything of the kind."[5]

But by New Year's Twain's debts were beginning to diminish, due in part to a plan for satisfying his creditors that Henry Huttleston Rogers, Twain's friend and financial adviser, had helped him devise. The gout was gone, and the family was settling in to life in Vienna. On January 14, 1898, Twain wrote in his journal: "Began to write comedy 'Is he Dead?' (François Millet.)" On January 20, Twain wrote Rogers, "Since we began to pay off the debts I have abundant peace of mind again—no sense of burden. Work is become a pleasure again—it is not labor, any longer. I am into it up to my ears, these last 3 or 4 weeks—and all *dramatic*. (I always believed I couldn't write a play that would *play*, but this one will that I am putting the finishing touches to.)" He had high hopes for success. "Yes," he continued jocularly, "I shall want seven rooms in the eleventh story of the new building next year, to conduct my dramatic business in. Please have them frescoed. Put in a billiard table. I will send you further details as they occur to me."[6]

Two days later, he wrote his friend William Dean Howells, "I have made a change lately—into dramatic work—& I find it absorbingly entertaining. I don't know that I can write a play that will play; but no matter, I'll write half a dozen that won't, anyway. Dear me, I didn't know there was such fun in it. . . . I get into immense spirits as soon as my day is fairly started." On February 5, Twain wrote Rogers that he had written a comedy entitled *Is He Dead?* "I put on the finishing touches to-day and read it to Mrs. Clemens, and she thinks it is very bully." Twain thought it was pretty good, himself.[7]

The play that lifted Twain's spirits so and that his wife found appealing as well (and she was hard to please in such matters) was not his first foray into the theatre. Indeed, *Colonel Sellers*, the very successful 1870s stage version of Twain's first effort as a novelist, had whetted his appetite for the stage and prompted him sporadically over the next two decades to try, and repeatedly fail, to follow it with another hit. But this time it was different. Twain knew that the play he had written was great fun and he wanted it to be produced. The London *Times* reported on February 4, even before Twain had added his "finishing touches," that *Is He Dead?* was to be "produced simultaneously in London and New York"—an idea that most likely came from Twain himself, reflecting the confidence he had in the play. Twain's friend Bram Stoker, author of *Dracula*, agreed to be his theatrical agent in England. But, much to Twain's disappointment, no theatre signed on. *"Put 'Is He Dead' in the fire,"* Twain wrote Rogers at the end of August 1898, frustrated by Stoker's and Rogers's failures to find a theatre that would produce it. "God will bless you. I too. I started in to convince myself that I could write a play or couldn't. I'm convinced. Nothing can disturb that conviction." But three months later he wrote Rogers, "It would be jolly good if some one should succeed in making a play out of 'Is He Dead?'"[8]

It never happened. Twain doesn't seem to have known that he had sent his play to Stoker to place in a theatre in England at precisely the moment when Stoker suffered a cataclysmic disaster that left him completely distracted. And Twain only partly realized that he had missed the boat, writing *Is He Dead?* just a few years too late. His play might have been snapped up by a theatre in the early 1890s, had Twain written it then, since it resembled, in some ways, the play that became the biggest worldwide theatrical hit of the decade. But by 1898, the theatre climate had changed on both sides of the Atlantic, and Twain's play was out of step with the latest fads. The play's irreverence toward an iconic figure in the arts, Jean-François Millet, may also have given some producers pause at a time when the "cult of Millet" in the United States was at its peak. Twain gave up trying to get the play produced a year after he wrote it.[9] It remained unprinted and unproduced for a hundred and five years.

Scholars have known about *Is He Dead?* but have paid it scant attention.[10] Twain's reputation as a dull playwright helped bury *Is He Dead?* alongside his other efforts in the dramatic field—most of which are well worth burying. Indeed, it was only after slogging through an entire file drawer of boring, largely unreadable plays, including the egregious *Ah Sin* and the deadly *Death Wafer*, that I came across the manuscript of *Is He Dead?* The fact that others had read Twain's last full-length comedy before and seen little remarkable about it prepared me to dismiss *Is He Dead?* with a quick perusal. But after laughing out loud in the archive, I found myself wondering, instead, why critics hadn't recognized the play for what it was—an engaging and (for Twain) unusually well-plotted comedy energized by the sly wit and insouciant humor Twain was able to muster when he was having a good time.

Is He Dead? marked the end of a period in Twain's writing life characterized mainly by fitful false starts and relatively few finished pieces in any genre.

During the productive twelve years that followed, Twain published works including "My First Lie and How I Got Out of It" (1899), "Concerning the Jews" (1899), *The Man That Corrupted Hadleyburg and Other Stories and Essays* (1900), "To the Person Sitting in Darkness" (1901), "A Dog's Tale" (1903), *My Début as a Literary Person, with Other Essays and Stories* (1903), *Extracts from Adam's Diary* (1904), "King Leopold's Soliloquy: A Defense of His Congo Rule" (1905), "The Czar's Soliloquy" (1905), *Eve's Diary Translated from the Original MS* (1906), "Hunting the Deceitful Turkey" (1906), *What Is Man?* (1906), *The $30,000 Bequest and Other Stories* (1906), *Christian Science* (1907), "Chapters from My Autobiography" (1906–1907), *Extract from Captain Stormfield's Visit to Heaven* (1909), and *Is Shakespeare Dead?* (1909). He also wrote works that were published posthumously, including "The War Prayer," "Battle Hymn of the Republic (Brought Down to Date)," "The United States of Lyncherdom," "The Stupendous Procession," "Corn-Pone Opinions," "The Fall of the Great Republic," "Which Was It?" "Adam's Soliloquy," "Eve Speaks," "The Dervish and the Offensive Stranger," "Three Thousand Years Among the Microbes," several of "The Mysterious Stranger" manuscripts, "Letters From the Earth," and a number of other works worth writing and worth reading.[11]

To allow the reader to experience *Is He Dead?* firsthand and to avoid giving away the plot, I will end my introductory remarks here. In the afterword, I set the play in the context of other writing by Twain (including his previous efforts to write for the stage), and other popular theatre of its time. I also examine Twain's attitudes toward art, and toward the French, and suggest why he may have chosen to write a play about the painter Jean-François Millet. I explore some possible reasons why he might have been unable to get it produced, and why a play that wouldn't play in the late 1890s might play today. For now, however, I give the reader *Is He Dead?*—the play that delighted its writer by proving to be "such fun."

SHELLEY FISHER FISHKIN

IS HE DEAD?

A COMEDY IN THREE ACTS

mark twain

TEXT TRANSCRIBED AND CORRECTED IN 2003 BY THE MARK TWAIN PROJECT
FROM THE ORIGINAL SECRETARIAL MANUSCRIPT WITH AUTHOR'S ANNOTATIONS
IN THE MARK TWAIN PAPERS, THE BANCROFT LIBRARY

Persons Represented.

Agamemnon Buckner, ("Chicago,") Young artist.

Jean François Millet, } Young artist.
Widow Daisy Tillou

Hans von Bismarck ("Dutchy,") Young artist.

Bastien André, picture-dealer and usurer.

Papa Leroux.

Sandy Ferguson, Young artist.

Charles Everest, Young artist.

Phelim O'Shaughnessy, Young artist.

Basil Thorpe, rich English Merchant.

Jared Walker, an Australian Wool-King.

Henry Parker, rich San Franciscan.

A young Turk. A young Hindoo.
} Pupils of Millet.
A young Spaniard. A young Chinaman.

Mother Leroux.

Marie, Millet's sweetheart.
} Young daughters of the Leroux.
Cecile, Chicago's sweetheart.

Madame Audrienne. Madame Bathilde. Madame Caron.

Some pretty girls, acquaintances of the young artists and pupils.

A gorgeous butler and several splendid flunkeys.

A page. A chimney sweep.

Memorandum. The handsome young gentleman (a bright Yale student) of whom "Chicago" is an attempted copy, was full of animal spirits and energies and activities, and was seldom still, except in his sleep—and never sad, for more than a moment at a time, awake or asleep. He had a singular facility and accuracy in playing (imaginary) musical instruments, and was always working off his superabundant steam in that way. He could thunder off famous classic pieces on the piano (imaginary) so accurately that musical experts could *name* the pieces. He imitated the flute, the banjo, the fiddle, the guitar, the hand-organ, the concertina, the trombone, the drum, and everything else; and for a change, would "conduct" a non-existent orchestra, or march as a drum major in front of a non-existent regiment.

If I have not made him a clean and thorough *gentleman* in this piece, I have at least strenuously intended to do it.

And I have intended Millet, too, to be a thorough gentleman, and the Widow Tillou to be a lady—a lady subject to accidents and mistakes and awkwardnesses in her unaccustomed costume, but still at heart a lady.   S L C

Note. The time is really before 1848, and Louis Philippe is still king. Millet was born before 1820 (I've forgotten the date, but it is not important.) In this piece he is about 25.

The sale of the "Angelus" by auction, to an American for 500,000 francs and France's re-purchase of it on the spot for 550,000 are events which occurred after Millet's death, but I have taken the pardonable liberty to highly antedate them.   S L C

Vienna, Feb. 21, 1898.

ACT I.

TIME—*not specified.*

PLACE—*Studio of Jean François Millet, at Barbizon, near Paris, lofty and spacious; faded and ragged sofa; cheap old chairs, several of them backless or otherwise crippled; other evidences of extreme poverty, to be imagined and furnished by the theater-management. Door R, front. Door L, front. A bedroom door in one of the walls. The walls are hung with two or three dozen framed chromos or something of the kind to represent oil pictures—the "Angelus" (covered) in the most prominent place, on a tall easel.*

Curtain exposes CHIMNEY SWEEP *sitting on a footstool, his head bowed on his knees, asleep. He gradually comes awake, yawns, stretches, looks around. Begins munching an apple.*

CHIMNEY SWEEP

No use waiting any longer. ——— I was behind time; now he'll say I didn't come.

(Gets up and stretches.)

Leave my card. It'll show I done his errand.

(Searches his soot-bag for card. Disappointed.)

Not a visiting-card left.

(Takes up a paint-brush—is going to paint his name on the canvas that covers the Angelus.)

Leave my name. ——— A-N ——— no, A-double-N ——— no—don't know how to spell it.

(Throws down brush. Sees the white sheet that covers the sofa. Nods approval. Stretches himself out on it. Rises and holds it up, exposing his printed form, done in soot. Hangs the sheet on the tall easel of the Angelus.) *(Exit, R.)*

(Enter DUTCHY—L.*)*

DUTCHY

If dot sweep ton't come, it mean he can't find him — — und dot would pe bad—*mighty* pad.

(Anxiously.)

I *vish* he vould come! I vish he — —

(Sees the sheet. Joyously.)

Goot! he's *peen* here — — — und it's all righd.

(Admiring the soot-print.)

Ah, dot is sphlennid—sphlennid, for a fellow dot hain't had no draining in Art.

(Turns the sheet clean-side up, and covers the ragged sofa with it.)

(Enter the LEROUX FAMILY—PAPA *and* MOTHER LEROUX, MARIE, CECILE, *and* CHICAGO. *Melancholy hand-shakings with* DUTCHY.*)*

*(*CHICAGO *is fidgeting around, the others sad. The* WOMEN *and the* OLD MAN *sitting.* DUTCHY *standing. The* LEROUX FAMILY *are cheaply and modestly but respectably dressed.* DUTCHY's *clothes show wear; he is clad in the ornamental cap, baldric, and high boots of a German college-corps student, and has a court-plaster X on his cheek from a recent duel.* CHICAGO *is neatly dressed as to cut, but his clothes are cheap and rather the worse for wear.* MARIE *is softly crying; has her head in* CECILE's *lap, who is stroking her hair.)*

PAPA

It's very hard. God knows I wish he would come, and let us know the worst.

CHICAGO

When is he due?

PAPA

By the noon train from Paris.

CHICAGO

Is it to collect the money?

PAPA

To — — to try to.

CHICAGO

Then he'll be on time.

PAPA

You know him?

CHICAGO

Do *I* know him? Well, I should think!

PAPA

Do you also owe him money? Are you in his grip?

CHICAGO

All of us. Millet, too.

DUTCHY

Py Chorge, François Millet he — —

CHICAGO

Oh, yes, *he* got in up to the chin. If he hadn't, we other young artists—
comrades and worshipers of his that swing round him and swim in his light
and warmth the same as the other planets up yonder swing round *their* sun—
would have starved, this year.

DUTCHY

Blanets ton't starve, dey ton't eat noding.

CHICAGO

Don't interrupt. Astronomical opinions based on sour krout are no good.

DUTCHY

(To no one in particular.)

Shecaggo he always yoost like dot. Always he ton't care for fact—only yoost boetry. Now of a blanet — —

CHICAGO

How much do you owe him?

PAPA

Ah enough to beggar me if he forecloses—fifteen thousand francs.

CHICAGO

Phe---u! How'd you come to get in so deep?

PAPA

It was wrong, it was foolish; but I did not know where else to go, and he was soft-spoken and smooth, and promised he would never press me. And now he as good as threatens to take the property.

DUTCHY

Oh, dot is noding. Of you haf his bromise in wriding — —

PAPA

But I haven't, I haven't. He was so smooth, you know, and he said — —

CHICAGO

All right, if he said it before witnesses, I guess you are safe. I wouldn't give up yet.

PAPA

But oh, dear, there wasn't any witness.

CHICAGO

Oh, hang it, that looks bad. It's an awful pity. Bastian André hasn't any heart in him. Carries a doughnut where it ought to be. Petrified one.

CECILE

That's the truth.

CHICAGO

Any picture-dealer is a hard enough lot; and when you add usury to it————! Well, what is he so sudden about, all at once?

MOTHER LEROUX

Marie has refused him again.

MARIE

I didn't love him.

CHICAGO

Oh, I see. That is, you all *suspect* that that is it.

CECILE

No, dearie—more than that. He *says* it.

PAPA

Here is his letter. Read it for yourself.

CHICAGO

(Mumbles it over.)

M---m. Well yes, it is pretty plain. M---m. Proposes once more. If the answer is "No," there can be "unpleasant results." What a low down scoundrel he is!

DUTCHY

I will jallenge him. I will job a sword troo him.

CHICAGO

A sword, you pretzel—they don't use swords in French duels, they fight with hair-pins — — — — hair-pins at thirty yards.

(Knock.)

Come in!

(Enter ANDRÉ, *R.)*

ANDRÉ

(Hesitating and apparently not pleased.)

I desired a private interview—and would prefer it if I may suggest—

CECILE

It is not necessary. These are friends.

PAPA

Please let them be no hindrance.

ANDRÉ

You got my letter?

PAPA

(Agitated.)

Yes. It was so sudden—so unexpected—so—so—it found me unprepared

(Rising and appealing to him.)

—I am sorry, deeply sorry I am not able to—to—but you will give me time, I know you will not be hard. You know you said — —

ANDRÉ

Said? *I* said? Pray what did I say?

PAPA

That you would not press me.

MOTHER

Yes, I remember it—he told me about it at the time. Be good, be kind, dear Monsieur André, the times are so hard for him, now; and he—well, you see, he was depending on your kind promise, and—

ANDRÉ

Please do not complicate the matter with imaginary promises—

PAPA

Imaginary!

MOTHER

Oh!

CECILE

Why, you ashcat!

ANDRÉ

It is the word I used, I believe. Come, now, let us drop this. Be reasonable. Look at the matter in a rational way; and surely you must see — — — — On the one hand a lover with nothing; on the other a lover who is getting on, with sure strides. I love your daughter as well as he does; I can give her a comfortable home, I can make her happy. He—can he do that?

CECILE

But man, where her heart is — —

ANDRÉ

This lad of 25 years—this unknown painter, this—this—François Millet, or Miller, or Milton, or whatever his name is—I *never* can remember it—Can he do that, I ask you? He can't sell a picture to save his life—he can't *give* one away.

DUTCHY

Wy, dot is *your* fault.

ANDRÉ

And he is in debt besides—head over heels in debt—absolutely hopelessly in debt. He owes *me* 2500 francs. If she marries me, *your* debt is paid. I tell you I am prospering. ——— Come—you will not throw me aside for this shiftless painter—this youth without talent or a future. Speak.

(Pause.)

PAPA

It is hard; it is very hard, to put it in that way. It is not for me to ———— Answer him, child.

MARIE

No, father, no. You will spare me that.

(Suppressing emotion.)

You shall answer him, and it shall be as you decide.

PAPA

There, dear—I know where your heart is. She has answered you, sir.

MARIE

No, father—don't put it so. How can I make a beggar of you? I can't bear it.

PAPA

My child, answer me this one question—only this one. Do you love this man?

MARIE

No.

PAPA

One more, then. Do you love François Millet?

MARIE

Yes.

PAPA

Well enough to endure poverty and hardship for his sake?

MARIE

Oh, hunger, thirst, cold, everything!

PAPA

She shall have her way – – Mother?

MOTHER

Please God she shall. We endured it in our young day.

PAPA

And were happy, too.

MOTHER

That we were!

PAPA

You have your answer, sir.

CHICAGO *(Plays imaginary trombone.)*

DUTCHY

(Approvingly, to both OLD PEOPLE.*)*

Shake!

(Shakes hands fervently.)

ANDRÉ

And you shall have mine. Your time is up day after tomorrow, 6 p.m., and I foreclose. Get the money in the meantime if you can!

CHICAGO

Come, no sass here.

ANDRÉ

Excuse me, I was not talking to you.

CHICAGO

But I was talking to you.

ANDRÉ

(To MARIE.*)*

Miss, I wish to make just one remark to you—

CECILE

Please let her alone. My father has answered you—now go.

ANDRÉ

It doesn't become *you* to ride the high horse—nor any of you. Paupers! everything you've got is mine—bought with my money. The very clothes you wear; if you took off what belong to me, there wouldn't be enough left to—

CHICAGO

There, you'd better go, now—you are about to get excited. Allow me

(With a bow.)

—show you the way.

(Leading him by the ear—or by the arm—choose for yourself.)

DUTCHY

Allow me.

(With bow. Puts ANDRÉ*'s plug hat on him and presses it down over his eyes.)*

Run along to your mudder, now.

ANDRÉ

(Putting his head back in at door.)

You'll hear from me again—all of you.   *(Exit—R.)*

MARIE
(Goes to her parents, who caress her.)

I'm so sorry, so sorry.

PAPA
Tut-tut! There—there, forget all about it.

CHICAGO
(Imaginary accordion—sings.)

'Mid pleasures and pala – – – –

(Imaginary drum—marching. Stops. Glances about. Says earnestly and inspiringly.)

Cheer up – – – cheer up—the worst is yet to come!

CECILE
Do be quiet, Agamemnon.

DUTCHY
(Piously.)

Dot name – – – du leeber Gott!

CECILE
There's nothing to be cheerful about, goodness knows.

CHICAGO
Don't you believe it, honey. I've written to every foreigner on the Paris hotel registers—they'll be flocking down here presently—

(Sweep of the hand toward the pictures.)

—we'll sell this whole exhibition in an hour. Come, nobody's going to starve.

MARIE
Do let him be cheerful if he can. I'm sure it does *me* good.

Sell! Sphlennid good pictures, but you can't *sell* 'em, no more'n brickbats.

CHICAGO

Oh, you'll see.

(To CECILE.*)*

Sweetest of the sweet, dearest of the dear—

(Drops his arm around her waist, she thrusts it away.)

CECILE

Don't! ——— Not before everybody.

(Billing and cooing between them. He attempts a kiss—she raps him.)

CHICAGO

(Reproachfully.)
Dearest—you always act like that when I kiss you in public.

CECILE

I *don't!* I mean *you* don't.

CHICAGO

Don't what?

CECILE

Kiss me in public.

CHICAGO

Well, now is that any of my fault?

CECILE

I wasn't saying it was anybody's fault. Fault? It's a crime, that's what it is.

CHICAGO

(Placidly.)

Oh, is that all? I don't care for those. Hey, the mourners are assembling.

(Elderly ladies begin to file in, sadly, R. Enter MESDAMES AUDRIENNE, BATHILDE, *and* CARON. *Grayheaded, and aged from 55 to 65. Comfortable folk of small tradesman class, no style, no fashion. Chord or two on non-existent banjo—sings softly to himself, while going to bow in and welcome the visitors, with* DUTCHY.*)*

"Buffalo gals won't you come out to-night, won't you come out to-night – –"

(The OLD LADIES *shake hands with everybody, and cry a little over the family. They don't sit down.* DUTCHY, CECILE *and* CHICAGO *group themselves apart; by-play; they do not hear what follows.)*

MADAME AUDRIENNE

We have just met that skinflint, and he told us all.

MADAME BATHILDE

And we came straight to carry you off and comfort you.

MOTHER

It is ever so good and kind of you. It's a hard day for us.

MADAME CARON

He says he is coming here presently to see young Millet—and he made threats.

PAPA

What did he say?

MADAME CARON

He wasn't very definite, and—

MADAME BATHILDE

He was definite enough about *two* things. He said young Millet owes him a pile of money and if he doesn't pay the cash he will have the law on him, and will spoil this exhibition besides.

PAPA

How?

MADAME BATHILDE

Oh, I don't know. Play some mean trick or other, I suppose.

MARIE

How cruel! Why, I don't see how anybody could be so unfair as that.

MADAME AUDRIENNE

Oh, *you* couldn't; but dear me, child, when you come to know the world better – – – Come, all of you—I've a bite waiting for you at home, and we'll talk it all over and you'll feel the better for it. Come while it's hot—everybody!

(Filing toward the door.)

CHICAGO

That means me.

(Moving.)

CECILE

Of course—as far as the word goes. There's hardly enough of it to describe you.

DUTCHY

(Stepping ahead and joining MARIE.*)*

Ton't you be drubbled, Marie, we all got to haf dese little up and towns, but dey don't last.

(Accompanies her to the door.)

MARIE

It's good of you to say so, Hans. You are always good.

(Exit all except DUTCHY *and* CHICAGO.*)*

CHICAGO

(Examining the Angelus.)

I tell you, Dutchy, this is the Koh-i-Noor of the whole collection.

DUTCHY

Yes, dot picture *spheak*—she yoost spheak!

CHICAGO

Ah it's great! That's the true word for it—great!

DUTCHY

(Laying hand on his heart.)

She make me *feel*—here. Dot pring pack Chermany—it pring pack *home*. Wenn I look at dot picture

(Putting his hand to his ear, listening.)

'vay off—'vay off yonder I hear de church bells—so fine—so faint—und so sweet—und dot is *home*, und dot preak me de heart.

CHICAGO

You've hit it! I don't know much about Catholic countries, but it makes me feel just so myself. That's the grand test—that's great art—and great art, supreme art, has no nationality.

DUTCHY

Oh, dot is *so*, Shecaggo. Dot picture she lif' me righd up to heaven!

CHICAGO

Look at the noble simplicity of it! No fuss, no feathers, no tricks of color, no theatricals; just that solemn half-light, and those brooding distances for the chimes to wander through, and those two humble figures, so poor outside, so rich with the peace of God in their hearts. Dutchy I'd rather be the painter of that picture than — — — look here, that picture's going to make a strike to-day—you'll see.

Py cracious I hope so.

CHICAGO

Hope it? I *know* it. I'll bet you François Millet's a celebrated man inside of a year. Come, put up!

DUTCHY

But I ton't want to pet against dot. I vant it to happen.

CHICAGO

That's the way to *make* it happen. Haven't you any superstitions?

DUTCHY

Shecaggo, you righd. Always wenn I pet agin somedings, she win, efery-time. How much we pet?

CHICAGO

Hundred francs.

DUTCHY

Take it.

(They search all their pockets, and lay out knives, pipes, matches, corkscrews, pawn tickets, and various rubbish.)

DUTCHY

I hafn't got dot much.

CHICAGO

My fix, too. How much you got?

DUTCHY

Fifteen sous.

(Piling them up.)

Me, to a centime.

(Piling them up.)

I call you. Who'll hold the stakes?

DUTCHY

It—vell, it is uncertain times.

CHICAGO

I understand. You'll hold yours, I'll hold mine.

DUTCHY

It is petter so. It could come one of dese financial grises. The paper say de reserve in de Bank of England is down to thirty-four million pound.

CHICAGO

No!

DUTCHY

The paper *say* it.

CHICAGO

It'll send the exchange kiting. What the nation are we coming to? Say— how'll we fix the rest of the bet?

DUTCHY

Can't we make a wriding?

CHICAGO

That's it.

(Writes.)

"Agamemnon Buckner bets the remainder of one hundred francs—being 95 francs 5 sous—15 sous being already put up in specie ('specie's' *good!*)— that François Millet will be a celebrated man within 12 months from to-day, and Hans von Bismarck bets the same against it." There, I'll give you a copy of it to-night.

(Looking off.)

Here are the boys.

*(Enter the 4 PUPILS in the dress of their nations. Also FERGUSON, EVEREST and O'SHAUGHNESSY. The clothes of all are rather shabby and worn.)**

Fall in! Attention! Now boys, prepare to receive the visitors and transact business. Fasten onto them—hang to them—don't let anybody get away without buying a picture at *some* price or other. Get two hundred francs for the small minor pictures when you can—take less when you must—but *sell.* Strike higher on the important ones. We're hard up—the wolf's at the door—but when this sale is over we are going to be flush and out of trouble. We'll make Bastien André wish that when he contracted with François Millet for these pictures he'd stuck to his bargain. When he sees the Angelus — — — —

EVEREST

He'll wish he *had* stuck.

(Murmur of assent.)

O'SHAUGHNESSY

That's so.

CHICAGO

Now that's our grand stand-by, boys.

(Takes a pin or two out of his lappel, while talking, and pains-takingly pins up a hanging rag of O'SHAUGHNESSY's coat—stepping back once or twice to view the effect, then doing the pinning again. Or this can be done by another.)

---

* [Author's note:] The Spaniard should wear faded blue velvet trimmed with tarnished silver lace. In the last Act both velvet and lace should be bright and new. The other 3 should wear damaged and faded <u>princely</u> costumes. In the last Act the same costumes, but new and splendid.   S L C

If everything else fails that'll save us. You want to get 2500 francs for that masterpiece.

(Murmur.)

Somebody give me another pin. O, I know it sounds big, but no matter. It's worth it, and don't you let it go for less. Answer to your names. Sandy Ferguson.

FERGUSON

Here!

CHICAGO

Collar the Presbyterians! This is a holy war. In holy wars holiness has never had a place. Rob them!

FERGUSON

I'm gaun to do it.

CHICAGO

Charley Everest!

EVEREST

Here!

CHICAGO

Take charge of your tribe—let no Englishman escape.

EVEREST *(Nods.)*

CHICAGO

Phelim O'Shaughnessy!

O'SHAUGHNESSY

Here, sor!

CHICAGO

Beguile the ladies.

O'SHAUGHNESSY

It's me trade.

CHICAGO

Alfonso de Alcantara y Salvador de Toledo!

ALFONSO *(Courtly bow.)*

CHICAGO

Assist O'Shaughnessy. Mohammed Ali ben Omar!

OMAR *(Salaam, spreading hands abroad.)*

CHICAGO

Li-Hung-Chang!

CHANG *(Chinese bow.)*

CHICAGO

Juggernaut Jamboree!

JUGGERNAUT *(Hindoo salaam.)*

CHICAGO

Assist the crowd!

CHANG

Me makee alle buy—Englishman, Ilishman, Mellican-man—makee alle buy. No buy, say "Go helly!"

CHICAGO

He's got the making of a Christian in him. Spread to your several places, lads.

(They spread.)

Dutchy, you are door-keeper and police. Stand by—it's train-time from Paris.

(Enter, CROWD of all sorts of people. Also ANDRÉ and several of his PALS. Also a lot of long-haired young LATIN-QUARTER ARTISTS, who shake hands with the BOYS. All move about examining the pictures, the BOYS with them explaining and conversing, O'SHAUGHNESSY devoting himself to the ladies. During the exhibition people are always coming and going—news-boys, flower girls, hand-organ players, peasants, laborers, mechanics, women with bundles, babies, baskets, etc. . .)

ANDRÉ
(Aside to PALS.)

Look sharp—break up every sale.

(They nod.)

BASIL THORPE
(Before the Angelus—ANDRÉ within earshot.)

Dear me, that looks good. I wish I knew something about pictures.

(Turning to EVEREST.)

Beg pardon did you speak to me?

EVEREST

I was only saying it IS good.

O'SHAUGHNESSY
(Trying to sell another picture—a PAL there to spoil the trade. To a lady.)

Indade, your ladyship it's worth the double of it—on me honor.

BASIL THORPE

Seems so to me, but I am no judge. The artist's name—I can't keep the name in mind.

(To a Scotch customer.)

Look at the grace of it, the charm of it! Ah ye'll no get the like of it for *that* money this side o' the grave.

EVEREST

No, not N — — M. Millet—François Millet.

THORPE

Miller. I don't remember — — —

EVEREST

Not Miller—Millet.

THORPE

Oh thanks. Franklin Millet. I — — —

EVEREST

François Millet.

THORPE

Thanks again. It looks very good. Do you think he will become known?

DUTCHY

(To a customer for another picture.)

For dot picture? Gott im Himmel!

EVEREST

Without a doubt. Not a doubt in the world. That picture will be worth a thousand pounds some day—maybe more.

THORPE

Dear me! Well I've heard of such things. But one can never tell when it's going to happen. I wonder what its price is.

CHANG

(To a customer of his.)

You go helly!

EVEREST

(Hesitating—pulling up his courage.)

Er – – – three thousand francs.

(Aside.)

Makes me gasp!

THORPE

(Musingly.)

I've a mind to take it. I've a mind – – –

O'SHAUGHNESSY

(To a lady.)

Why, bless the dear heart of ye, the *canvas* cost more!

EVEREST

(Aside—excited.)

He's landed—I've got him, sure! By Jove our troubles are over and old Millet's safe!

THORPE

Yes – – I *will* take it.

EVEREST

(Aside.)

O, Lovely!

THORPE

Tell me, young man, how do you know it's a good picture?

Because I am an artist myself.

(Glancing suspiciously.)

Perhaps — — — Are *you* Mr. Milton?

I? Millet? *No*, sir.

Oh,—pardon. No harm meant young man—don't take it amiss.

(To a customer.)

Oh, indeed, no—it's worth every penny of it.

It grows on me — — — grows on me. If—well, if I could get it for 25 hundred—

(Too eagerly.)

I—I—I—I believe you can, sir.

(Suspiciously.)

Are you personally interested in the sale of the picture?

(Vexed with himself but concealing it.)

Yes, sir, in this way, and to this degree—that Mr. Millet is a very close friend of mine, and whatever concerns him interests me.

Oh, I see. That's all right. Right and quite natural. Well, if he were here and would take 25 – – –

FERGUSON

(To a customer.)

I'll no say but that if ye'll mak it 275 it's a trade.

(One of the PALS *mixes in.)*

EVEREST

May I go and ask him, sir?

THORPE

(Suspicious again.)

Well, n-no – – I'll think it over a little! I'll think it over a little, first. Still you might mention it to him—not as an *offer*, you know, not as an offer, but just a—

EVEREST

I'll be back in a few minutes, sir.

(To O'SHAUGHNESSY *as he goes along.)*

Take a grip on yourself and don't let your feelings make a noise. I've as good as sold the Angelus—in fact I know I *have* sold it, for – – – hold your grip I tell you—twen--ty-f-i-v-e hundred francs!

O'SHAUGHNESSY

Mother of—

EVEREST

(Putting hand over O'SHAUGHNESSY's *mouth.)*

Quiet, you blackguard! Tell the boys.

(Threads the crowd and disappears.)

(The news spreads from mouth to mouth of the CONSPIRATORS *and the* PUPILS—*great excitement—dumb show—hand-shaking, embracing, health-drinking, etc. . .)*

ANDRÉ

(To THORPE.*)*

I beg pardon—Lord Palmerston, I believe?

*(*THORPE *pleased.)*

No, I see my mistake—deceived by the strong resemblance. I have never seen him, but his portraits are everywhere, of course. I have had the honor of buying many pictures for his lordship's collection.

THORPE

Then you know pictures?

ANDRÉ

Yes, it is my business to know them.

THORPE

Would you mind telling me what you think of this collection?

ANDRÉ

Well,

(Pause.)

some of the frames are very good.

THORPE

Frames!

ANDRÉ

But they are borrowed—borrowed from the dealers. The artist has struggled manfully—I must say that for him—but where there is such lack of talent—

THORPE

He lacks talent, does he?

ANDRÉ

Oh, not utterly—not altogether, but ———. I tried to help him. I offered to take all the pictures he could turn out in a year, at a hundred francs apiece, provided they came up to a certain standard. Well, here is the result.

(A glance around the place.)

Three reached the standard; the rest are failures—as you see.

THORPE

What, aren't these worth a hundred francs apiece?

ANDRÉ

The frames, yes—but as I told you—

THORPE

But *this* one?

ANDRÉ

This one is better. It really has a glimmer of merit. It was not painted strictly within the time-limit, or I believe I should take it.

THORPE

At a hundred francs?

ANDRÉ

Yes. In fact I think it is worth four times that.

THORPE

(Glances around, sees EVEREST *coming.* EVEREST *stops to pass a word with one of the* BOYS.*)*

Excuse me, sir; I have an engagement. *(Exit.)*

(To a customer.)

Well, then, suppose we say 750 for the 3?

(Enter CHIMNEY SWEEP.*)*

CHIMNEY SWEEP

(With his brushes and bag, standing in front of the Angelus and munching an apple.)

They call *that* Art!

(Moves away, inspecting other pictures disapprovingly.)   *(Exit.)*

A PAL

(Indicating several pictures.)

(To CHICAGO.*)*

Now that—and that—and those others—would you take 1500 – – – if – – –

(Arguments in dumb show—another PAL *detaches the other customer and rids the place of him.)*

ANDRÉ

(Aside. Crowd is leaving during this time.)

Ah yes, Monsieur Millet, you have your sweetheart—and next you'll have hunger and a raging good appetite. Day after tomorrow I'll drop on you; then there'll have to be an auction—I'll buy all these for a song – – and *burn* them—and you're a ruined man. You've painted good pictures—yes, they're all good. But this—ah, this one's almost *great!*

CHANG

(To a customer.)

You go helly.

FERGUSON

(To a customer.)

All right. It's really worth a good deal more, but — —

(ANDRÉ interrupts to speak to him, and a PAL gets the customer away and goes out talking with him. Other people drifting after, ANDRÉ joining the last that leave. Strangers all gone. Long pause.)

O'SHAUGHNESSY

(Grieved.)

Not a single picture sold!

FERGUSON

It's the most mysterious thing. I as good as sold 300 francs worth.

O'SHAUGHNESSY

And I the double of it.

DUTCHY

I yoost the same, py cracious.

EVEREST

And that Englishman. Well, I had to let on to go and consult—and by Jove it cost us just 25—hundred—solid—francs! Think of it!

CHICAGO

I had a customer for 3 pictures at about 700, and another for 6 at 1500—one got away and the other finally backed down. — — — Ruined — — — ruined! — — — *Can't* understand it!

CECILE

It's a shame!

(Long silence; sorrowful attitudes.)

(Starts to play imaginary flageolet—gives it up. Says sadly—)

Cheer up—the worst is yet to come. — — — — Here's François Millet!

(Enter MILLET. MARIE *goes to him.)*

MARIE

You've been *so* long!

MILLET

I'm glad it seemed long to you, sweetheart. Well, lads, how — — — but you needn't tell me. — —

(Enter ANDRÉ, *R.)*

Monsieur André?

ANDRÉ

I suppose you know what I have come for?

MILLET

For instance? — —

ANDRÉ

My twenty-five hundred francs.

MILLET

In what way do I owe you 2,500 francs?

(Darkness of evening beginning to come on.)

ANDRÉ

Haven't you borrowed it of me?

MILLET

No, sir, I took it on account.

ANDRÉ

On what account?

MILLET

On account of the year's pictures. There they are. You have persistently refused them. That is not my fault. We have tried to sell them and pay you your
money. I perceive that we have failed. Take the pictures—take them along.

ANDRÉ

I don't want them.

MILLET

That is not my affair—I hold you to your contract.

ANDRÉ

The contract leaves me free to take such as I like, and leave the rest. I take
none of them.

MILLET

Free?

ANDRÉ

I will read it to you. "It is hereby agreed between the undersigned that
Bastien André may take all the pictures painted by François Millet from
and after this date for the space of one year, the price to be 100 francs a
piece for the same." He *may* take them. Anything there about *shall?*

MILLET

No there isn't. But that is nothing. I called your attention to that, at the
time.

ANDRÉ

To what?

MILLET

I *told* you it ought to say shall, and you said contracts between gentlemen didn't need such refinements.

ANDRÉ

I said it, did I? And what did *you* think?

MILLET

I thought the same.

ANDRÉ

What do you think now?

MILLET

I still think it.

ANDRÉ

Ah, you are very witty. You remember my saying that, do you?

MILLET

Clearly.

ANDRÉ

Well, I don't. Perhaps you can furnish a witness?

MILLET

There was no witness.

ANDRÉ

Then if you please we will drop this imaginary rot. I give you just 48 hours to pay that money in, or I'll—

MILLET

You are forgetting yourself, Monsieur André, you have just used an expression which you will need to modify. That presently. Meantime I make you this offer. Take all the pictures, including the new one, and call the account square. The Angelus has merit.

ANDRÉ

I decline.

MILLET

Very well.

ANDRÉ

Months ago you stepped between me and – – no matter about that, I'll tell you frankly I made up my mind to make you sorry for it. And I'll do it. I'll ruin you – – understand?—ruin you.

LADIES

Shame!

MILLET

Now to the expression which you used. It is time for you to take it back.

ANDRÉ

(Snaps fingers.)

That's for you and your – –

(MILLET springs for him, but the others crowd him aside and bundle ANDRÉ out at the door. Puts his head in and says—)

Two days to pay the money in—remember that! (Exit.)

(Pause.)

EVEREST

We are ruined.

MILLET

Yes; that is the word.

FERGUSON

Yet for a while it looked so promising.

MILLET

(Sad.)

Ah, well, it's no matter now. It is all over. All these years I have done what a man might to – – – to – – I have worked hard – – – faithfully – – – – – I am a tired man.

MARIE

Don't give up, François, don't give up.

MILLET

I have spoiled *your* life, dear. That is the hardest.

MARIE

No you have blest it. Don't give up—for my sake. Oh François I wish I could help you. I would die for you.

MILLET

I believe it.

(Aside.)

And so I will die for *her*. Then some good fellow with the gift of success in him will save her and she will be happy.

DUTCHY

Look at dot Angelus! It is a fool world—*always*. Wen it haf a creat Master, it ton't know it—und let him starve. Und ven he is tead, und it is too late, his name fill de whole worl', und de riches come!

O'SHAUGHNESSY

Bedad it's a true word.

It *is* a true word. It's just the world's way.

And it's a shame, too. And it's going to happen when our old Millet is gone.

(Goes and shakes hands with him.)

François you've been the best friend to us boys that ever — — — ever — — — —

(Emotion—walks away, with bent head, unconsciously doing a few bars on a jewsharp.)

Night is come.

Yes, we must go.

(Shakes hands with MILLET.*)*

I am sorry for you, poor lad, God knows I am. If I could only help—but the man has ruined me, too.

Bless you for a good heart.

*(*MARIE *takes leave of* MILLET.*)*

(To MILLET.*)*

God be with you, lad. Come to us in the morning.

(Passes on with MARIE, DUTCHY, O'SHAUGHNESSY, FERGUSON *and* EVEREST *following.)*   *(Exit, these.)*

EVEREST

(Speaking back.)

We'll see them home, and come back.

(CHICAGO and CECILE follow in the rear.)

(Exit, CECILE.)

(The foreign pupils sit with bent heads in melancholy attitudes. MILLET drops into a chair and bows his head in his hands.)

CHICAGO

(Glances back—returns and lays an affectionate hand on MILLET's shoulder, and says haltingly and with emotion—)

Ch-cheer up—the worst is − − −

(Can't finish.)   *(Exit, blowing nose.)*

(Pause; lights turned low.)

MILLET

(Gets up and thinks—passing his hands through his hair—looking around on the motionless group. Aside.)

It is better so

(Lighting candle.)

− − − I was so hopeful—once. − − But—it is all so − − − − so − − − − not worth while.

(Closes the doors and lights a charcoal fire in the brazier.)

Boys!

(They look up.)

Say good-bye to me—and go.

(Nods toward the brazier.)

I see. I thank you for that good thought. Say good-bye to us, lads.

THE TURK

We have nothing to eat—then how shall we live? Kismet. −− It is written. I remain also.

CHANG

Welly good. Flançois welly good fliend to Li-Hung-Chang. I no leave Flançois. He die, I die, too.

(All shake hands, and dispose themselves to die. As the fumes gather and spread, they show the effects—sitting up for a moment, gazing around dazed, confused—putting hands to head, heart, throat—moaning—gasping— struggling for breath—lying down again. Finally, long, dying gasps.)

CHICAGO

(Bursting in. Most of his clothes gone, and he is covered with snow.)

Hurray, boys we're saved, we're saved! −− Hel-lo, what's this!

(Rushes and throws water on brazier and spreads doors open. Working at MILLET.*)*

Wake up—wake! Oh, don't die—we're saved, I tell you, we're saved!

(Enter FERGUSON, DUTCHY, EVEREST, O'SHAUGHNESSY.*)*

ALL OF THEM

Heavens!

(They get to work on the PUPILS *and gradually bring them round.)*

MILLET

(Speaking feebly and with difficulty.)

Ah, lads, why have you done us this unkindness? So that we may die by inches, of hunger?

CHICAGO

No *sir*, not any die, by a long shot. We are going to live, and be happy.

EVEREST

Live? Live on what?

FERGUSON

What are you driving at?

MILLET

Happy? We are perishing. I've kept it dark, but I haven't tasted food since—

CHICAGO

Well, you *will* taste it. The minute we left here I struck an idea.

DUTCHY

Py chings you look like it.

O'SHAUGHNESSY

Where'd you disappear to, when you left us?

EVEREST

Yes, what went with you?

CHICAGO

Keep still and let me tell you. I tell you I struck an idea. I left you fellows to see the people home, and broke for the monte di pietà at the end of the village and spouted my coat and vest and necktie.

DUTCHY

Call dot an idea!

(*Enter* WAITERS, *bringing food, beer, cigars, cigarettes. Then Exit* WAITERS.)

CHICAGO

—And here's the result! I haven't come to my idea yet. Wait, and eat. I tell you we're saved!

(The BOYS *fall to, hungrily. After a time of silent gorging — — — .)*

MILLET

It tastes *so* good! I have to forgive you.

THE SPANIARD

Ah never was anything so good.

DUTCHY

Now den, 'poud dot idea.

FERGUSON

Out with it!

EVEREST

Fetch it out!

CHICAGO

It isn't my idea at all. It's Dutchy's.

DUTCHY

How is dot?

CHICAGO

(Seriously. Rising.)

It's this. No use for us *all* to die. One's enough. Let one of us die, to save the rest.

(Pause.)

Dutchy said, "When there's a great Master, the people don't *know* it—and they let him starve; and when he is dead and it is too late, his name fills the whole world, and the riches come."

(Pause.)

One of us must *seem* to die—must change his name and disappear—we'll make his name sound through the world, and the riches will come.

(Raising his glass in left hand.)

François Millet must die!

DUTCHY

Py cracious it is yoost sphlennid! — — — *Shake!*—

(Shakes with CHICAGO.*)*

EVEREST

(Jumping up.)

Three and a tiger for our benefactor, Chicago!

ALL

(Springing up except MILLET. *They give him the 3 and a tiger—Sing.)*

For he's a jolly good fellow, for he's a jolly good fellow,
For he's a jolly good fellow, which nobody can deny.
Which nobody can deny, which nobody can deny,
For he's a jolly good fellow, for he's a jolly good fellow,
For he's a jolly good fellow, which nobody can deny.

(They sit down—except CHICAGO.*)*

CHICAGO

(With genuine feeling and solemnity.)

Friends, you will drink, in silence and standing.

(Pause, while the others solemnly rise and stand with bent heads—two or three that had their hats on uncovering.)

To the sacred memory of him who was always our stay, our comfort, and our refuge in time of distress—the best friend that ever man had in this world —— the late Jean François Millet, who sleeps in peace, God rest his soul!

(Toast drunk in silence.)

(Curtain—slowly.)

ACT II.

TIME—*the next day but one.*
PLACE—*The Studio Again.*

*Half of the pictures, including the Angelus, are gone. Half that remain are plac-
arded "SOLD" in big letters. In the most prominent place, on easels, two good-sized
pictures. One of them ("the Sowers,") is finished, the other (for the* WIDOW *to work
at) is roughly begun.*

Everybody present is dressed as before, except that CHICAGO *wears a shabby coat
and necktie of different color from those he left at the pawn-shop. The coat is close-
buttoned, for he has no vest. He is pains-takingly sewing a vast white or bright yellow patch into the seat of a pair of old blue pants.*

(Present the 5 YOUNG ARTIST-FRIENDS *and the 4* FOREIGN PUPILS.*)*

The PUPILS *stand at easels, painting. The* YOUNG ARTISTS *move from easel to
easel, instructing, pointing out defects, sometimes taking the brush and making
corrections—with now and then a remark; they presently gather around a pupil.
Rather large picture of a Dachshund—visible to audience.*

EVEREST

That dog's not right.

FERGUSON

He's all out of drawing.

O'SHAUGHNESSY

No sir, that's no Christian dog. I never saw a dog like that.

EVEREST

He's too long.

O'SHAUGHNESSY

It *is* a mighty long dog. It's the longest dog I—why, I never saw such a long dog.

FERGUSON

He's like a bench.

DUTCHY

You kwyde righd. Dot dog want foreshortening.

O'SHAUGHNESSY

What kind of a dog *is* it, anyway? Is it a *real* dog, or only a *design* for a new kind of dog?

PUPIL

It's a dachs.

EVEREST

Oh, that accounts for it.

O'SHAUGHNESSY

But he's got too much tail, anyway—he never could wag it.

EVEREST

No the tail's all right. They're always made that way, now. It's a good deal too long but it has to be so, to harmonise with the rest of the dog.

FERGUSON

Why? You just said it's too long—so it's out of proportion. How's it going to harmonise?

EVEREST

All the details of that kind of a dog are out of proportion—they have to be, to harmonise.

FERGUSON

Oh—I see.

DUTCHY

I ton't care, it ain't any way to make a dog. A tail like dot is not becoming to a dog. A tail like dot, dat hang down und lay on de ground, und get in de dog's way wen he want to turn around — — —

EVEREST

Well, hang it, how are you going to better it?

DUTCHY

(Reflectively.)

I—I ton't know. — — B-but you could bend it up over—so—und tie it round his neck, und—

CHICAGO

O, shucks! you don't know as much as an art-critic.

(Holds up the pants—exposing the patch—views his work critically.)

(Aside.)

Failure — — too loud — — can't wear them — — — distract attention from the rest of the exhibition — — — make a person look like a lightning-bug—*

(Puts the pants down—gets up and stands with hands on hips viewing the arrangement of the pictures on the walls.)

That looks good—looks first-rate. However — — — I believe it would improve it to sell a couple more.

---

* [Author's note:] I couldn't do what I originally meant to do with those pants—strike them out entirely, if you want to. Their main function was to emphasize the poverty of the boys.   S L C

DUTCHY

(Ready, with old step-ladder and placards.)

Well, wich ones, do you dink?

CHICAGO

That one—and that one.

DUTCHY

All righd.

(Placards them.)

"SOLD."

FERGUSON

Yes, that's better.

CHICAGO

Seems to me, Sandy, we better sell that one there, too.

FERGUSON

Good.

(Placards it.)

"SOLD."

EVEREST

Look here, Chicago, what shall we say has become of the others?

CHICAGO

I've been thinking it would be a good idea to say a dealer who got the news out of the evening papers yesterday came last night and pretended—er— pretended—

DUTCHY

Dot he had an order from somepody und—

CHICAGO

That's it; and carried them off at 300 francs apiece, but the Widow—well, what does the Widow say?

DUTCHY

Well, she say—

(Reflecting.)

— — — suppose she say it is a fraud und she get them pack again py de law.

CHICAGO

That's all right—that'll do. It's no slouch of a cabbage you carry around on your shoulders, Dutchy.

DUTCHY

(Pleased.)

Oh, Shecaggo, you always flatter somepody, hain'd it?

EVEREST

Chicago, how did you manage about that item in the papers?

(Showing it to one of the BOYS.*)*

CHICAGO

Remember Flandreau?—Beaux Arts, two years ago—couldn't make painting go? Journalist, now—knows all the guild; he worked it for me.

FERGUSON

It's worded just right—cautious, not over-done. It's doing its work. I was in Paris this morning. People are talking.

CHICAGO

That's good. What do they say?

Not one man would let on that he was hearing François Millet's name for the first time.

Now *isn't* that human nature? Isn't it?

All over. And they're all so sorry that the poor fellow is ill—

Ill and had to leave yesterday morning for—for—where is it?

Barbary coast.

Where is the Barbary coast?

Hanged if I know.

Well then, what did you put it in, for?

Had to go *some*where, hadn't he? Muggins!

Several people made out that they had regarded Millet as the rising great master this long time. Asked if he was as ill as the papers said. When I said he could not possibly live many weeks, they said his death is going to be an awful blow to France.

Splendid!

FERGUSON

Oh, it's working. There'll be people down here to-day to buy. You'll see.

CHICAGO

They'll *pay* for what they get—I can tell you that. Say—

EVEREST

What?

CHICAGO

I got it worked into the Paris Correspondence of the London Times.

ALL

No!

CHICAGO

Well, I did.

O'SHAUGHNESSY

Lon-don Times! It'll wake up the whole world!

(*Knock. Enter* 4 REPORTERS, *with note book and pencil and begin to take off overcoats.*)

CHICAGO

(*Aside.*)

Reporters! oh, jolly! Distribute them. All of you help load them up—but merely repeat what you hear *us* say.

REPORTER

Could you give me a few details about this deplorable thing?

CHICAGO

Ah, the poor fellow—I suppose you had heard of him before?

REPORTER

(Hurt.)

Dear sir, I hardly expected that you—you—Surely the representatives of a journal like Figaro could hardly be charged with being unfamiliar with the name of Jean François Millet.

CHICAGO

I beg a thousand pardons. If I had known you were from Figaro, I ――― Perhaps you would like a little sketch of his life and—er—achievements.

O'SHAUGHNESSY

(Aside.)

Achievements is *good!*

REPORTER

I should be infinitely grateful—infinitely!

CHICAGO

(Giving it him.)

It is but a little thing—jotted down last night—tribute of a breaking heart.

DUTCHY

(Aside—lifting hands and wagging head.)

Oh, dot Shecaggo—he always loaded.

REPORTER

(Glancing over the document.)

Um. Has no family but a widowed sister. Sent for and arrived night before last, in time to bid him what was without doubt a last fare-well. Sad.

CHICAGO

Yes. Widow Tillou. Poor thing—poor thing. Utterly broken down—you never saw anything like it.

EVEREST

She will occupy his quarters, here, and attend to his affairs.

CHICAGO

By the way—the first thing she learned when she arrived was that her brother had been defrauded.

REPORTER

Please tell me about it.

CHICAGO

Just before she came, a rascal who pretended to be a brother of the noted and excellent dealer, Bastien André—

DUTCHY

(Aside and softly slapping his thigh.)

Sphlennid, sphlennid.

CHICAGO

Came here with a forged paper entitling him to 25 pictures at the beggarly price of 300 francs each.

EVEREST

We supposed it was all right, and took the money and let him carry them away.

FERGUSON

Didn't notice that the paper was false until too late.

REPORTER

Scandalous! I will ventilate the thing.

CHICAGO

Do. It will insure their return.

EVEREST

We shall all be grateful.

O'SHAUGHNESSY

And the widow, of course.

REPORTER

Is there anything else?

CHICAGO

I believe not—because all the rest is in the obituary—I don't mean that—in the little paper I gave you. Oh, would you mind saying that for the present the widow has decided to sell none of the pictures at any price except four.

FERGUSON

Could you mention that?

DUTCHY

   (Aside.)
Oh, dot Shecaggo!

REPORTER

With pleasure.

   (Glancing at walls.)

I think that too many have been sold already.

CHICAGO

Quite right. We could have sold a hundred just as easily as we have sold those.

FERGUSON

But we hope to get the most of them back again by paying a good bonus.

REPORTER

I hope you will succeed, but I very much doubt it. *I* know the world.

CHICAGO

(Aside.)

Yes, you look it.

REPORTER

I suppose I could not see the widow?

CHICAGO

Yesterday afternoon she could have seen you—she was almost cheerful for a while—almost hopeful and had her portrait sketched in black and white—but to-day, alas — — — !

REPORTER

Oh, pray! could I borrow that for reproduction in Figaro?

CHICAGO

(Gives him the picture.)

Ah, with pleasure.

REPORTER

It is a most striking face—a most engaging and remarkable face.

CHICAGO

Yes. And exactly like her poor brother—exactly. They were twins.

DUTCHY

(Aside.)

Dot Shecaggo!

REPORTER

Thank you *very* much indeed.

(Indicating the easel-artists.)

These are—

Pupils of the master. Of course there are others, but these were his fa-
vorites. Kept them under his immediate eye. Allow me.

(Helps him on with his overcoat. The BOYS *accompany him and the other*
REPORTERS *to the door and bow them out.)*

(Exit REPORTERS.*)*

CHICAGO

(Marching—beating drum.)

Say—Dutchy—I've got a little bet with you, you know.

DUTCHY

Dot bet ton't begin to look so bromising any more. But I'm clad of it.

(The WIDOW *(young, handsome, cheaply but prettily dressed with hat or*
without it, as you please,) comes mincing out of the bedroom, smoking a
corncob or briarwood pipe.)

CHICAGO

Hi, you mustn't come out here!

(To the BOYS.*)*

Jump for that door—don't let anybody in!

(The BOYS *obey.)*

Come, Millet, back with you—it's dangerous.

WIDOW

Hang it, Chicago, have some pity—I can't stand it in there.

CHICAGO

O, but you must.

WIDOW

(Walking up and down.)

Ah, this is good.

(*Yawning and stretching.*)

It's so stuffy in there—no room to turn around.

(*Before the new picture.*)

I want to go on with this one.

(*Takes up brush.*)

EVEREST

(*Pleadingly.*)

Oh, come, you'll ruin everything.

WIDOW

Why, I've *got* to have some air. And that bedroom's the worst place to paint pictures in—there isn't any light. I can't turn out anything but daubs—it's impossible.

CHICAGO

Oh, turn out what you dern please—we can sell them.

WIDOW

How long have I got to paint pictures in there?

CHICAGO

Oh, 3 months.

WIDOW

You assassin!

FERGUSON

But you've got to. The thing's bigger than we dreamed of.

WIDOW

I can't endure these awkward clothes.

CHICAGO

O, you'll have to. You must turn out a raft of pictures. Rattle them off—anything will do.

WIDOW

Nonsense.

CHICAGO

We've got to have them, I tell you—not for now, but to sell after you're dead.

WIDOW

Oh, I want to die now.

CHICAGO

But you can't. We can't afford it.

EVEREST

It'll take 3 months to spread your fame all over the world.

CHICAGO

Then you can die.

WIDOW

(Despondently.)
I'll never live to — — — to do it.

FERGUSON

Yes you will, old boy, don't you worry.

CHICAGO

Now you mark my words—three months from now we'll give you the biggest funeral that ever—

(Patting him on the shoulder—persuasively.)

—a funeral that you'll enjoy.

Oh, — — 3 months!

CHICAGO

(Lifting his hand—impressively.)

And the minute you are dead you'll see the pictures jump to 50,000 francs a piece—you mark my words.

WIDOW

(Turning, and catching a glimpse of the walls.)

Oh, Christmas!

DUTCHY

(At door.)

Jump! Some-pody's coming. It's dot rich Englishman.

(The WIDOW *gathers up her skirts and flies into the bedroom.)*

(Enter the ENGLISH MERCHANT. *The usual* MISCELLANEOUS CROWD, *too?)*

CHICAGO

Look sad, boys. Remember we're in deep affliction.

*(*ALL *run to door and look off.)*

FERGUSON

My wool king from Australia—

CHICAGO

And my nabob from San Francisco—and a lot more.

DUTCHY

Sell some of dese people, now, ain'd it?

(Each receives his man sadly and goes off with him—dumb show of disputing.)

CHICAGO

(Aside to BOYS.*)*

Put the prices away high, and don't close without getting my assent as the Widow's agent.

ENGLISHMAN

(A little anxiously, to EVEREST.*)*

I was sorry to be called away so suddenly, but it's all right, I've brought the money.

(Fumbling in his pocket-book.)

WOOL-KING

(To FERGUSON.*)*

The 275 francs, as agreed upon—

(Fumbling in pocket-book.)

FERGUSON   *(Dumb show of dissent—dispute.)*

NABOB

(To CHICAGO.*)*

I believe it was 1500 francs.

(Fumbling in pocket-book.)

CHICAGO   *(Dumb show of dissent—dispute.)*

EVEREST

(Trying to remember.)

Er—what money do you refer to?

ENGLISHMAN

For the picture I bought, you remember.

EVEREST

Picture?

ENGLISHMAN

Yes. The Angelus, you know.

EVEREST

Oh, I remember, now. It's sold.

ENGLISHMAN

Sold?

EVEREST

I think so. The agent will know. The Angelus is sold, isn't it?

CHICAGO

Sold? No. You mean the affair this morning?—agent of the Emperor of Austria?

EVEREST

Y-yes.

CHICAGO

Merely an *offer*—30,000 francs. Declined.

DUTCHY *(Dumb show expressive of "Dot Shecaggo!")*

(The ENGLISHMAN *and the* WOOL-KING *move to* CHICAGO.*)*

ENGLISHMAN

Good heavens!

NABOB

Thir--ty thousand?

WOOL-KING

My word!

ENGLISHMAN

But my dear sir, the picture is in effect mine—I would have taken it on the spot, only—

EVEREST

Only you didn't close, you remember.

ENGLISHMAN

Because a gentleman whom I heard called André—I think that is the name—advised—

EVEREST

(Aside.)

That explains it.

(The same in dumb show by the OTHERS.*)*

(Indifferently—aloud.)

Oh, André—that was all right, in the way of business. André's a picture-dealer.

ENGLISHMAN

Well, aren't picture dealers honest?

CHIMNEY SWEEP

(Enters eating apple and contemplating "Sowers" with contempt.)

S'more Art!

(Wanders around. Then examines "Dachshund" with approval.)

THAT's something LIKE! *(Exit.)*

EVEREST

(Regretfully.)

There have been some.

CHICAGO

(Regretfully.)

Dead, now.

ENGLISHMAN

Now only day before yesterday these pictures were going at—

CHICAGO

Yes, I know. But two or three very important things have happened since, and the situation has changed.

FERGUSON

Yes. The greatest painter of modern times is suddenly threatened with death.

EVEREST

The values go up, by consequence.

CHICAGO

And still another change. Day before yesterday his sister the Widow Tillou, was in poverty. She has now come into sudden possession of an enormous property.

O'SHAUGHNESSY

(Aside.)

That's no lie, the way things are looking up.

CHICAGO

Her orders are positive. I can sell four pictures and no more.

ALL

Which are they, please?

CHICAGO

That—that—that—and this masterpiece, which will soon be famous throughout the world—"the Sowers."

ENGLISHMAN

What is the price?

CHICAGO

I cannot entertain an offer short of 30,000 francs.

THE BOYS

(All over the room, softly—)

Phe-ew!

DUTCHY

(Aside.)

O, dot Shecaggo! Got more cheek as an angel.

ENGLISHMAN

It's an im — —

NABOB

I take it—30,000!

WOOL-KING

I *raise* you . . . . 32,000!

ENGLISHMAN

Thirty-five!

NABOB

Forty!

WOOL-KING

Forty-five!

ENGLISHMAN

Fifty!

NABOB

(Hesitating.)

F-fifty-five!

WOOL-KING

Gentlemen, calm yourselves. We are simply butting our own brains out, here. It's not business. I'll throw dice with you who's to have it at 60,000 francs, if the machinery is here.

ENGLISHMAN

That is fair.

NABOB

All right.

(Dice produced.)

WOOL-KING

(Throws.)

Aces! Oh, Hell-ifax!

NABOB

(Throws.)

Aces! Amster--*dam!*

ENGLISHMAN

(Throws.)

Aces!

(Throws again.)

Double fives!

(Throws.)

Double-fives! It's between you and me, sir, I guess. I'll give you 10,000 francs to draw out.

ENGLISHMAN

N-no.

NABOB

Give you fifteen.

ENGLISHMAN

(Going and examining the picture.)

No.

NABOB

Twenty. Come!

ENGLISHMAN

(Glancing at the picture—hesitating a while.)

I'm English. I'll stand to my guns.

WOOL-KING

P'raps you'd like to buy *my* chance, gentlemen?

NABOB

(Humorously.)

Why certainly. Ten francs.

ENGLISHMAN

Ten and a half!

NABOB

Eleven!

ENGLISHMAN

Twelve!

NABOB

And a half!

ENGLISHMAN

Going—going—last call. Thir- - -teen!

NABOB

(Sorrowfully.)

You've raised me out.

ENGLISHMAN

Here's your thirteen.

(Proffering money.)

WOOL-KING

O, where I come from we never go back when we start in. Not for thirteen francs.

(Rattling the dice.)

Our country's coat of arms has on it *"Advance,* Australia!"

(Throws.)

(Tableau. ALL bend over the dice.)

NABOB

Double sixes! For the honor of America I'll give you 65,000 for the picture.

WOOL-KING *(Shakes head.)*

ENGLISHMAN

For the glory of England—seventy—

WOOL-KING *(Shakes head.)*

NABOB

Seventy-five.

WOOL-KING *(Shakes head.)*

ENGLISHMAN

Eighty.

WOOL-KING

No use—in our country we never go back.

CHICAGO

(Waving toward the picture.)

Advance, Australia!

NABOB

Now this little picture which I was to have had for 700 francs—

CHICAGO

Day before yesterday.

NABOB

And to-day?

CHICAGO

Ten thousand. Five minutes to decide in.

NABOB

Ten? It seems to me—

ENGLISHMAN

I'll take it.

NABOB

Excuse me—I'll take it myself. I hadn't finished.

ENGLISHMAN

Very well. How much for the other two?

CHICAGO

Ten thousand a piece—if you hurry.

NABOB

I'll — —

ENGLISHMAN

I take both!

WOOL-KING

(Has been drawing a cheque.)

There's your 60,000—payable to bearer.

CHICAGO

That's right.

(Takes it.)

WOOL-KING

Now, paint on the back of the picture—I'll dictate. "This picture of the Sowers has this day been sold to Jared Walker for 60,000 francs, money down—receipt hereby acknowledged—is sworn to be a genuine Jean François Millet, and stands second in rank of the master's creations." Sign it. Put the date. Now put under it, "Advance, Australia."

CHICAGO

(Accompanying him to the door.)

You have made a grand bargain, sir. The picture's worth more than that.

I should *say* so seeing I've just been offered 80,000 for it. *(Exit.)*

(Meantime EVEREST *and* FERGUSON *have received cheques from* NABOB *and* ENGLISHMAN *and written on their pictures. Accompany them to door—dumb show.)*

(Exit BOTH.*)*

(The PEOPLE *who have been drifting through the studio have all gone.)*

CHICAGO

(Marches—imaginary drum.)

Now then. Hip-hip-hip –– hurrah! Hip-hip-hip-hurrah! Hip-hip-hip –– hurrah! *Tiger!*

*(Embrace—dance—*PUPILS *and* ALL.*)*

CHICAGO

(To O'SHAUGHNESSY*—giving cheques.)*

Deposit these 90,000 francs in the village bank to the credit of the Widow Tillou—and bring back a cheque-book.

O'SHAUGHNESSY

Ninety thousand—think of it! Bedad if I had a drum and fife to go wid me!

CHICAGO

And SAY—for goodness sake bring back a cigarette. I'm dying for a smoke.

O'SHAUGHNESSY

I'll do it. Give me the money.

CHICAGO

(Searches his pockets.)

(To the CROWD.*)*

Got a couple of sous?

(Passes from one to another.)

You?—You? You?

(They all search and shake their heads. To O'SHAUGHNESSY.*)*

Well, go on—never mind.

O'SHAUGHNESSY

(Starts out—turns again.)

Chicago!

CHICAGO

Yes.

O'SHAUGHNESSY

The bank'll have to have three or four samples of the widow's signature.

CHICAGO

That's so. Wait—I'll get them.

(Starts toward bedroom.)

(Enter from it the WIDOW.*)*

WIDOW

What was that noise about?

EVEREST

Quick! Jump for that door, boys. Don't let anybody in.

WIDOW

My, but it's good to get out of that place for a minute!

CHICAGO

SAY, Widow, we've sold 90,000 francs' worth of pictures!

(Falls, knocking down an easel—is gathered up by the BOYS.*)*

What a lie! What do you want to knock the breath out of a person with such rubbish as that, for?

EVEREST

It isn't rubbish, old man, it's true.

WIDOW

What do you mean? Gone mad? Ferguson?

FERGUSON

Honor bright, it's true.

WIDOW

Dutchy, you are the only man here that's had any practice in speaking the truth. Tell me.

DUTCHY

It's the gospel truth, Widow—it's yoost what it is.

WIDOW

(Putting his handkerchief to his eyes—soliloquising.)

After all these hardships — — — these privations — — — —these miseries — —

(Looking up.)

Den of thieves and liars! You ought all to be taken out and drowned—every last one of you.

CHICAGO

I — — I hadn't anything to do with it.

(Murmur.)

WIDOW

Why, nobody was accusing you — — you Chicago lamb.— — — You conscience-
less robber! What did you do it for, you rascal?

CHICAGO

Well you see, we—well we hadn't any cigarettes, and—

WIDOW

O, I see. It's all right—I didn't think of that. Come to my arms O, noble
scoundrel!

(Embracing.)

Bless your heart, I couldn't disapprove of you. I know I should go on loving
you and forgiving you if it had been a *hundred* thousand.

CHICAGO

I thought of making it that.

WIDOW

I haven't a doubt of it.

CHICAGO

Why, three months from now I wouldn't take twice the money for those
pictures. You'll see. But we're depositing the money—you'll need a cheque-
book. Here—knock off a few sample-signatures.

(Giving pen.)

WIDOW

It's wonderful. Seems impossible. I've never had to do with a bank in my
life. Let me see—what is my name—my given name?

CHICAGO

Suggest something, boys.

Alice.

Don't like it.

Lily.

It's what they call housemaids.

Antoine.

It's a man's name, you ass.

Daisy.

That's the ticket.

I like it pretty well. Do I look it?

You bet!

All right, Daisy it is.

　　(Writes.)

"D-a-y —— " Do you spell it with a z?

O'SHAUGHNESSY

No—no. Nor a y. D-a-i-s-e-y.

FERGUSON

Leave out the e.

WIDOW *(Writes a dozen.)*

CHICAGO

(Examining.)

Sho! no two alike. Here—this is the best one. Make some more like it. — — —

WIDOW *(Does it.)*

CHICAGO

— — — These will do very well. Keep a copy, so that you will know how to write it next time.

(To o'shaughnessy.*)*

Run along.

*(*o'shaughnessy *takes them, and exits.)*

DUTCHY

Und so he can tell it, when he sees it again.

O'SHAUGHNESSY

(Putting head in at door.)

Look out, the old people are coming down the road.   *(Exit.)*

WIDOW

(Scared.)

Stop them. Put them off, again.

No-no. It won't do. We had difficulty yesterday. They'll get suspicious.

EVEREST

We promised positively for to-day.

FERGUSON

Said you'd be clear over your prostration.

WIDOW

O pity. I haven't got the hang of these clothes yet. They'll see that I'm not a woman.

DUTCHY

Poys it's so. It's tangerous.

WIDOW

You see I'm femininely ignorant. I could make fatal mistakes in talking.

CHICAGO

Good! That's the idea. I'll tell them you are eccentric—very eccentric— maybe a little crazed by this great sorrow. See? The wilder you talk the better it will be. Come!

WIDOW

(Reluctantly.)

Very well, I'll do the best I can. But some of you get out, now, and then the rest as soon as I'm introduced. I can't stand too much of an exhibition. Let me run in and fix my hair. *(Exit.)*

(All except CHICAGO, DUTCHY, FERGUSON *and* EVEREST *file out L. as the* OLD LADIES *file in R.* CHICAGO *locks the door.)*

MADAME AUDRIENNE

It is good of you to let us come. We do so want to see the poor dear, and be of some help if we can. How is she to-day?

CHICAGO

Physically, entirely restored, I am glad to say. But ———

(Tapping his forehead.)

(Piteous murmurs and gestures from the OLD LADIES.*)*

CHICAGO

Yes. It was a heavy blow you see.

FERGUSON

Her mind seems to be a little touched.

MADAME BATHILDE

Oh, not seriously, I hope.

FERGUSON

No, it's a mere trifle and will soon pass.

MADAME CARON

Ah, that is good.

EVEREST

It merely makes her seem a little awkward in handling herself.

CHICAGO

And sometimes her talk sounds a little—er—extraordinary—that is to say, a little—er—*unusual*, perhaps—but it's really nothing when you ——— 'sh, she is coming.

(Enter WIDOW.*)*

(Privately to OLD LADIES.*)*

She's a little bit stiff in one leg, yet—please don't notice it. Madame Tillou, I have the pleasure and the privilege to present to you some very dear old friends of your brother's.

WIDOW

I am so grateful.

CHICAGO

Madame Leroux.

(BOTH *curtsy.*)

(*Aside to* WIDOW.)

Just a *leetle* more style.

CHICAGO

Madame Audrienne.

(BOTH *curtsy.*)

(*To* WIDOW *aside.*)

That's better. Madame Bathilde.

(BOTH *curtsy.*)

(*To* WIDOW *aside.*)

Noble! Madame Caron.

(*Curtsy.*)

(*The* BOYS *dumb show of hearty greeting and chat—while they seat the* WIDOW *and the* OLD LADIES *in a group.*)

CHICAGO

(*To* WIDOW.)

We will leave you a moment with these good friends, Madame, but shall be back almost at once.

*(*ALL *seated.)*

MOTHER LEROUX

(Taking widow's *hand in both of hers fondlingly, for a moment.)*

Ah, dear Madame, that he should be gone so far from us—and to die—
to die! we love your poor dear brother so.

MADAME AUDRIENNE

Ah, indeed yes!

WIDOW

(Touched—his voice makes the women start.)

It goes to my heart to hear you say these sweet words.

MOTHER LEROUX

Your poor brother's very voice—how lovely!

MADAME BATHILDE

And the face—why, it's almost the very image!

MADAME CARON

Not quite so broad, but wonderfully like!

MOTHER LEROUX

The hands, too—almost exactly the same, though his were a trifle smaller.
He had a great pink scar just above his wrist, and many a time—

*(She is going to examine—*widow *gets his hand away and fumbles his chin.)*

MADAME BATHILDE

Oh, you are *so* like your poor dear brother!

WIDOW

We are twins.

MADAME BATHILDE

Ah, that accounts for it—though you look considerably younger than he.

WIDOW

Yes, I—I am the youngest.

MADAME AUDRIENNE

Youngest?

WIDOW

Oh, nothing to speak of. He was born on a Monday morning and I—I think—
I th — — yes, I was born the next Saturday night.

MOTHER LEROUX

Goodness!

MADAME CARON

(Aside.)

Poor thing, her mind *is* touched.

WIDOW

I do not remember it myself. I used to, but I don't now. Years and years ago
I got hit here—just about here.

(Touching top of head.)

And it injured my memory; and so, since then I can't remember it at all, I
only remember that I *used* to remember it.

MOTHER LEROUX

How very extraordinary.

WIDOW

Yes, as I was saying, years and years ago I got hit—just here—by an Irishman—

MOTHER LEROUX

The brute!

WIDOW

Oh, he didn't mean it—it wasn't intentional. I was passing along the sidewalk, and he—er—he fell off the roof—he was at work up there, you know—and I wasn't noticing, and he struck me just there—there, you, you can feel if you like—

(The OLD WOMEN *feel his head.)*

—and then he bounced off like that

(Circles in the air with hand.)

—summersaults, you know—a most providential escape—

MADAME AUDRIENNE

Won-derful. The hand of Providence—

WIDOW

In it?

(Impressively.)

Plain—plain. If I hadn't been there that Irishman would have been killed.

MADAME AUDRIENNE

Oh – – – The Irishman!

WIDOW

Certainly he would. Said so himself. It made a changed man of him. He reformed.

MADAME CARON

Reformed?

WIDOW

Yes—from acting like that. Signed the pledge.

MOTHER LEROUX

The pledge?

WIDOW

Yes. Agreed to break himself. He told my first husband—no, not the first. Another one. Pierre. – – Well, it was one of the early ones, anyway. Yes, he told him – –

MADAME AUDRIENNE

Dearie, how old are you?

WIDOW

Twenty-five.

MADAME BATHILDE

And had so much experience. It is wonderful. Have you had any children?

WIDOW

(Indifferently.)

Slathers.

MADAME AUDRIENNE

(Dazed—aside.)

Slathers.

MADAME BATHILDE

(Dazed—aside.)

Slathers.

MADAME CARON
(Dazed—aside.)

Slathers.

MOTHER LEROUX
(Dazed.)

Talks just as a rabbit might.

WIDOW

Seven in two years.

ALL

Seven!

WIDOW

Some in the spring, some in the fall, others along here and there—

ALL

My!

WIDOW

According to the weather.

MADAME CARON
(To MADAME BATHILDE, *privately.)*

I do believe her mind's touched.

MADAME BATHILDE

By another Irishman?

MADAME CARON

A whole colony of them.

MADAME AUDRIENNE

Did they all live?

WIDOW

(Handkerchief.)

Alas, none of them.

ALL

Poor thing!

WIDOW

All my poor nine darlings—

MOTHER LEROUX

Nine, dear? You said seven.

WIDOW

(Weeping.)

I speak of another vintage.

MADAME BATHILDE

What a singular name for it.

WIDOW

I remember, now, there were several. Edmond—poor dear little Edmond—he made a brave struggle. He remained longest. Ah, the sweetest angel. The pick of the first litter.

MOTHER LEROUX

(Aside.)

Talks *just* as a rabbit might.

MADAME CARON

(Aside.)

Nothing can ever persuade me that her mind isn't touched.

MOTHER LEROUX

Were they—

WIDOW

Boys and girls? Some of them—yes.

MOTHER LEROUX

Some of them? Weren't they all?

WIDOW

Many thought so.

MADAME AUDRIENNE

What did *you* think?

WIDOW

At this late date I could not be certain, of course. Still, I think there was
considerable variety.

MADAME CARON

(*To* MADAME BATHILDE.)

She is certainly touched in her mind. It is not safe for her to be alone. One
of us must sleep with her to-night.

MADAME BATHILDE

You are perfectly right. Will you propose it?

MADAME CARON

You never can tell what a person in her condition will do. Like as not just
take a freak and object.

MADAME BATHILDE

Quite right—best to just act, and say nothing.

MADAME CARON

I think so. I wonder — — do you think she could become violent?

MADAME BATHILDE

I think not, but there's no telling. Perhaps I'd better come, too.

MADAME CARON

If you would be so kind. We could arrange with her agent, young Chicago, to let us in, and we needn't disturb her; we could spread blankets here on this floor—

MADAME BATHILDE

Good—and we should hear any noise that came from her room. We better come early.

MADAME CARON

(Nods approval.)

It's my opinion she's always been touched, and her brother didn't like to expose it. We were all saying to-day that he had never mentioned that he *had* a sister.

(Been growing dark.)

MADAME BATHILDE

I remember. That explains it all.

(Looking at watch.)

Night's coming on.

(Knock R.)

CHICAGO

(Entering, L.)

Coming!

(Speaking off at R.)

Cheque-book? All right. Go around the back way. You can't come in here.

(Returning, is intercepted by MESDAMES CARON *and* BATHILDE. *Dumb show of talk.)*

(Aside.)

It's just too divine!

(Aloud.)

Ah how kind of you. Would you be kind enough to speak to her about it?

MADAME CARON

You think it best?

CHICAGO

To speak to her? Yes, I think so. But at present, you know, she is full of whims, and if she should take the notion to object, it's best to humor her.

MADAME BATHILDE

No doubt your judgment is right—come Madame Caron.

(They precede CHICAGO *to the* WIDOW.*)*

MADAME CARON

Dear Madame Tillou would you like several of us to come and sleep with you to-night?

WIDOW

(Looks from one to the other speechless. Then aside.)

That's Chicago's work—I'll drown that fellow, yet.

(In CHICAGO'*s ear.)*

Get me out of this scrape—and go hang yourself.

CHICAGO

(Delivers check-book to WIDOW.*)*

(To MESDAMES CARON *and* BATHILDE *privately.)*

It seems to disturb her; I wouldn't push it. It's just as I told you, she's full of
the strangest whims. *(Exit, L.)*

MOTHER LEROUX

(To WIDOW.*)*

But as I was saying, dear, he was so prostrated by this trouble that I had to
leave him at home in care of the girls. And poor Marie so wanted to come
here with us! You will love her straightway when you see her, I know—for
his sake.

WIDOW

(Aside.)

For her own, too.

(Aloud.)

Tell me—let me get a clean, concise idea of the situation. To begin with,
what is your husband's first name?

MOTHER LEROUX

Pierre. Your poor brother must have—

WIDOW

Mentioned him in letters? He never wrote any—except a line now and then
to tell me of his health and enclose me a little money to live on. Dearly as
we loved each other there was a coolness. He couldn't get over it because I
didn't name all the children after him. I did name eleven of them for him—

MADAME CARON

(Aside.)

There, her mind's wandering again.

Then I quit. I said it was no use—he had an unappeasable appetite that way. Now then, go on and tell me in three words the amount of this debt, when it is due, the man's name, and—

MOTHER LEROUX

Fifteen thousand francs. He gave us till to-day. His name is André—Bastien André—picture-dealer and usurer.

WIDOW

It is a cruel and shameful thing. And you were old particular friends of my poor brother?

MADAME LEROUX

Oh, yes.

WIDOW

This must be looked into.

MOTHER LEROUX

Ah, if you only *could* persuade him to extend the time! Oh, if you only can!

WIDOW

*(Touches bell—*CHICAGO *appears.)*

Write a note to Mr. Erastus Anderson—

MOTHER LEROUX

Bastien André—

WIDOW

Pardon,—to Mr. Bastien André, horse-dealer—

MOTHER LEROUX

—Picture-dealer.

Picture-dealer, and say I wish to see him on a small matter which—

(Knock R.)

CHICAGO

(At door.)

It's the man himself.

WIDOW

Admit him.

(Enter ANDRÉ.*)*

ANDRÉ

(Aside.)

The Widow, I guess. Stunner! and just like her brother.

(To MOTHER LEROUX.*)*

Madame, I have just left the bedside of your husband, who says he is unable to pay. Now I have come to serve personal notice upon you that I allow you just—

(Looking at watch.)

WIDOW

(With aristocratic lassitude.)

Wait, please. You are disturbing my nerves. And your manner toward this valued old friend of my brother is uncourteous to her and an affront to me. One should not get excited over a pecuniary trifle—

ANDRÉ

Trifle, madam! When you come to know the amount you—

WIDOW

Peace! I know all about it.

(To CHICAGO—*lazily.)*

Draw this person a cheque for – – – um – – – ah, I remember, now— hundred and fifteen thousand francs—

CHICAGO

(Admiringly. Aside.)

'George, he's an artist!

MOTHER LEROUX

No! no! no! *Fifteen* thousand!

WIDOW

(To ANDRÉ, *with austere severity.)*

Fifteen thousand francs? Is that all it is?

ANDRÉ

(Humbly.)

That is all, Madam.

WIDOW

(To CHICAGO.*)*

Draw the cheque. Write a receipt in full for this person to sign.

> **MOTHER LEROUX**   *(Weeping; with French passion repeatedly kisses the hem of the* WIDOW*'s garment.)*

WIDOW

(To ANDRÉ—*pause—inspecting him critically.)*

Is it the custom of people in your line of business to go around in person to collect financial chicken-feed like this?

(Aside, to CHICAGO,—*taking pen:)*

What's my name?

(Whispering.)

Daisy. Here's the sample-signature.

WIDOW

(Signs two cheques, per sample—gives them to ANDRÉ; *gives the receipt to* MOTHER LEROUX.)

My brother owed you some money. Here it is. I don't want a receipt—the cheque-stub will answer. And here are the 15,000.

(Seriously.)

I wish to say a word to you,—then you may go. I ought to put it in strong language; but I am a lady and that privilege is denied me. From these friends I know your history. You are a man without pity—a man whose lust for money has withered every kindly impulse you were born with. You found my brother and his poor young artist-friends struggling honestly and manfully for their bread against hunger and misery, and you have traded upon their poverty;

(Gradually rising excitement.)

you have bought their pictures for francs, and sold them for Louis d'or, you have hidden their talents, such as they were, from the world,

(Rising from seat.)

you have beguiled them into debt and robbed them in a hundred mean and pitiful ways; and yonder, stretched upon his bed lies that blameless old man whom your deceptions, your inhumanities, your pitiless brutalities have brought there—

PAPA LEROUX

(Tottering in R. feeble, excited—appealingly.)

Ah, beg him to have mercy!

WIDOW

(With vehemence.)

I am a lady, and I know the limitations that are upon me, but this I *will* say—
that from head to heel, from heart to marrow, from pallet to midriff you are
a mean, cowardly, contemptible, base-begotten damned scoundrel!—oh!

(Turns away embarrassed.)

(Curtain descending.)

MADAME AUDRIENNE

(Reverently.)

Beau-tiful as a prayer!

MADAME CARON

(To herself.)

Mind's as sound as a nut.

ANDRÉ

I will have the pictures—I refuse the cheque.

(Tears it up and throws the pieces on the floor.)

Curtain.

ACT III.

TIME—*3 months later. Late afternoon.*
PLACE—*The* WIDOW'*s palatial drawing-room in Paris.*

WIDOW

(WIDOW *richly and tastefully dressed,—walking up and down smoking a pipe.*)

(*Solus.*)

After all these weeks Monsieur André's love-making begins to tire me a little. But it has been a mine of satisfaction to the boys, and a body can't refuse them anything. They want me actually to marry him—but I draw the line there – – – – I wonder how it would do to – – – to – – Of course I must get that forged contract out of him somehow or other, or he will seize and hold the 3 million francs, and we can't very well afford that—certainly can't afford to let *him* get rich out of us—oh no! – – – – Nobody but I can prove the document a forgery, and I can't do it without exposing our game and who I am. – – He's due now, and I'm not ready. – – – – Suppose I *promise* to marry him on condition that he—

GORGEOUS FLUNKEY

Monsieur André.   (*Exit.*)

(*Enter* ANDRÉ.)

(WIDOW *hides pipe.*)

ANDRÉ

(Kissing WIDOW's *forehead.)*

My precious!

(Aside.)

Phew! She's been smoking.

WIDOW

(Tapping him with her fan.)

Naughty boy! I suppose I ought to scold you.

ANDRÉ

(Puts his arm around her—she does not resist.)

Dearest if you would always be like this.

WIDOW

I will. Dear Bastien you have conquered me.

ANDRÉ

At last! O, this *is* bliss.

(Kisses her passionately several times.)

WIDOW

O, you frighten me! But—

ANDRÉ

But what, sweetest?

WIDOW

(Shyly.)

I like it.

You darling!

(*Kiss.*)

O, I could eat you!

(*Kiss.*)

WIDOW

Do you really love me, Bastien? Really and truly?

ANDRÉ

Love you? Oh, Daisy!

WIDOW

Do you love me well enough to—to—

ANDRÉ

To what, dear?

WIDOW

To make me forget that you ever said those cruel words to me.

ANDRÉ

About — — ?

WIDOW

The time you said if I didn't marry you you would carry my poor brother's contract into the courts?

ANDRÉ

I never meant it, darling—never, never. It was only a wild outburst of despair. Forgive me, precious. You do forgive me, don't you?

WIDOW

Forgive you? The moment you have made me forget it—oh, so gladly. But

you know, as long as that piece of paper exists to remind me of that cruel
hour—

ANDRÉ

(Kiss.)

It shall cease to exist the moment you promise to be mine. Here it is—
promise, darling, and take it.

WIDOW

(Takes it.)

I do pr — — — Let me—

(Mumbles it over. Aside.)

It's a capital forgery! Two witnesses,—pals of his, I suppose.

(Aloud.)

Poor brother! I suppose it was the last thing he did before he went away
to die?

(Puts the paper down.)

ANDRÉ

Almost the very last. Returned it to me by the hand of the witnesses. I had
been unkind and had refused the poor dear fellow's pictures. I was sorry
and ashamed, for he was really right in saying the old contract should have
read "Shall" the way this one does, and so I framed this one, dating it back,
and putting in the "Shall" and signed and sent it to him for his signature.
He was very grateful.

WIDOW

(Aside.)

The man's a mere moral abscess; by example I am getting to be another.

ANDRÉ

(Aside.)

She's just in the humor—a touch of the heroics will fetch her.

(Strikes a match.)

WIDOW

(Aside.)

It's a forgery, but I *can't* stomach it to procure the paper by these shady means.

ANDRÉ *(Fires the paper.)*

WIDOW

(Aside.)

I won't make the promise.

(Aloud—snatching the burning paper.)

What are you doing!

ANDRÉ

Too late, sweetheart—it's nothing but a cinder.

WIDOW

Ah, you noble creature!

(Aside.)

I've got him, sure! he never would have burnt it if he had had the courage to bring it into court.

ANDRÉ

O, Daisy, we shall be so happy together. Give me the promise, sweetheart, and make me entirely happy beyond all doubt or question.

(Aside.)

If I only had a chance to think up a way out! I must make a pretext to gain time.

(Begins to cry.)

Dearest! What is it?

O, think of the day!—I am wicked—I was forgetting it.

The day?

This day—my poor brother's funeral. To betroth myself and he—he— Let me wait a few hours and—

(A noise—voices, rearward.)

Run, dear—there are strangers in the house—you would not wish to compromise me.

(Hurried leave-taking.)

(Exit ANDRÉ.*)*

(Enter MARIE *in deep mourning—rear—pale and weak—puts hand on chair to steady herself.)*

Wait, dear, let me come and help you.

(Aside.)

It breaks my heart to see her suffer so.

(Goes and puts her arm about her and brings her slowly forward.)

There, dear heart, rest your head upon my shoulder.

(MARIE *cries.*)

Oh, I am so sorry for you. I wish I could comfort you.

(*Pause.*)

MARIE

Daisy?

WIDOW

Yes, darling.

MARIE

It is almost time for the funeral.

(*Sobs.*)

WIDOW

Bear up, dear heart. He is better off, now, than he was when he was alive.

MARIE

It is so consoling to think it. You *do* believe he is better off, *don't* you, Daisy?

WIDOW

O, I know it.

(*Pressing* MARIE *close.*)

Kiss me for his sake, dear.

(*Kiss.*)

MARIE

He couldn't be better off than he is now, *could* he?

WIDOW

(Kiss.)

Not imaginable.

MARIE

I love to have you kiss me, Daisy.

WIDOW

Do you dear?

(Kiss.)

MARIE

Yes. It's just the way he used to do it his own self.

WIDOW

Is it?

MARIE

Ex-actly. And he hugged me the same way—just ex-actly. It's wonderful. Isn't it strange?

WIDOW

I never could have believed it.

MARIE

Well, it's true, just as I tell you. You remind me of him in so many ways. You look like him, you act like him, you have his dear voice, you almost walk like him.

WIDOW

Do I?

MARIE

Indeed you do. He was more graceful; but in woman's clothes I think he wouldn't have been. I don't think he would have kicked his skirts around the way you do sometimes; still he might because he was an impetuous creature.

(*Aside.*)

Phew! I do wish she wouldn't smoke.

WIDOW

I am glad I remind you of him.

MARIE

Well, you do—oh, in so many many ways. All these three months it's been almost as if I was *with* him.

WIDOW

Yes?

MARIE

He used to forget himself and swear. You do that, Daisy. And it is very naughty. I think it is so strange. I've never heard any lady do it but you.

WIDOW

Well—er—I don't do it often.

MARIE (*Looks at him gravely—says nothing.*)

WIDOW (*Gets away from the look— looks away—whistles softly "Rory O'More."*)

MARIE

Daisy! You forget.

WIDOW

I? Forget what?

MARIE

The day.

WIDOW

The day?

MARIE

The funeral.

WIDOW

(Aside.)

O, hang the funeral. I can't keep it in my mind—I've never had one before.

(Aloud.)

No, I had not forgotten—I always whistle when I am sad.

MARIE

Well, that's one thing that's not like him—but it's almost the only one. Oh, he was so good, and tender, and kind. He had pity for *every*body that was in trouble, and would do everything he could to help them. I wish you were more like him in those ways, Daisy.

WIDOW

For instance?

MARIE

Well, you don't treat that poor Mr. André right, dear. He loves you, Daisy.

WIDOW

He's a bad man, and he tried to ruin your father.

MARIE

Yes, he is bad, but there is good in everybody, somewhere; and he has never had the right influences around him. It hurts me so, to see you keep him hopeful a week, and then miserable a week, and then hopeful again, and then — — — why, Daisy you know it's cruel. And Chicago—Chicago's always egging him on, and telling him you'll marry him yet, and it's *too* bad.

WIDOW

Would you like me to marry him, dear-heart?

MARIE

Y-yes—I would. Because it would uplift him, it would save him.

WIDOW

Why, you poor innocent, he's only after my money, that's all.

MARIE

Daisy! it's no such thing.

WIDOW

How do you know?

MARIE

Because he *told* me so.

WIDOW

That settles it.

MARIE

Well, then, may I send him word you are going to marry him? Do let me, Daisy.

WIDOW

No, I'll be d

(Her hand on his mouth.)

hanged if I will.

MARIE

Well, then, won't you put him out of his trouble?

WIDOW

I—er—I don't know about that.

MARIE

Do, dear Daisy—for my sake.

WIDOW

(Aside—musing.)

Cap-ital idea! I see my way out. Chicago can send out and buy the things and take the dimensions, and at 10 o'clock to-night—

(Aloud.)

Ah, well, I give in—I suppose if you were to ask me for my head I'd have to give it to you, dear.

MARIE

You darling sister!

(Kiss.)

WIDOW

I'll be alone in this room at ten to-night. Send him word to slip in here in a quiet way and unannounced. I'll give him his answer, plain yes or plain no.

MARIE

O, goody! And try to make it yes. He loves you, and I do pity him so.

WIDOW

Well, we'll see, we'll see. If he turns out to be really anxious—

MARIE

O, he'll be anxious enough—no question about that. You are so good, Daisy. You've made all of dear François' young fellows rich—how sweet that was of you! And they all worship you, just as they did him.

WIDOW

It's no merit in *me,* child, I did it for his sake.

MARIE

Don't talk so! It's more merit in you than it would have been in him,
a hundred times over; for they were his friends not yours.

(Solemnly.)

I worship the very ground you walk on, Daisy Tillou. $---$ Why do you
laugh?

WIDOW

I don't know; I always laugh when I'm touched.

MARIE

He didn't, he cried—I've seen him.

WIDOW

(Aside.)

I, too—or pretty near it.

MARIE

And he wasn't as—as—as queer as you, Daisy. He wouldn't be dressed the
way you are if it was *your* funeral.

WIDOW

(Sadly.)

I know; I'm made all wrong. I always dress so at funerals.

MARIE

O, have I hurt you, dear?

(Kiss.)

WIDOW

No, darling, no. But I'm not going to this one—I couldn't bear it.

MARIE

But dear, there'll be people here.

WIDOW

Only friends, who will understand; and strangers who won't know who I am.

MARIE

I hear voices now. I don't wish to meet any one—it's too sad.

(Kiss.)

(Exit, assisted by the WIDOW.*)*

WIDOW

(Returning—Looking from window.)

Ger-reat Caesar! – – – the whole Champs Elysées – – – – Clear to the Arch – – – just the cloven Red Sea, with the population of Paris for walls – – – – the walls fronted with soldiers standing elbow to elbow all the way – – – su-perb spectacle! – – – – the mile of houses swathed in black from eaves to pavement – – – – distant glint and sparkle playing about a black mass flowing from under the Arch – – – – wonder what it is? – – – Oh, bayonets! – – – stretches and stretches, grows and grows! – – – Lord, is the entire army—?

(Enter CHICAGO, *nobbily dressed—plug hat—crape scarf on arm.)*

CHICAGO

Old man, it's the grandest day! Oh, everything booming! Lemme hug you. Old boy, you're going to have the nobbiest funeral Paris has seen in fifty years, bar Napoleon's. Say, what are you doing in this rig? Aren't you going to attend it?

WIDOW

No I'm not. The idea of a man attending his own funeral. I never heard of such a thing.

CHICAGO

All right, but you're going to miss a good time.

(*Enter* EVEREST.)

EVEREST

Lord, François, if you could only go outside and mingle with the people and hear them talk!

CHICAGO

You can't imagine what it's like!

EVEREST

The whole nation is in tears.

CHICAGO

England, too, and the continent.

EVEREST

We thought we had piled your fame high enough before, but, my! since you died — —

CHICAGO

Ten days! only ten days! It's the most colossal jump that ever a reputation took in the world!

(*Enter* O'SHAUGHNESSY.)

O'SHAUGHNESSY

Boys, the King himself is going to the funeral!

ALL

'Rah!

(CHICAGO *marches, playing trombone, the other three dance to each other an Irish jig.* MARIE *appears in the distance—mute amazement—disappears.*)

O'SHAUGHNESSY

And the Sultan of Turkey and the two other visiting monarchs!

ALL

'Rah!

O'SHAUGHNESSY

All the foreign Ambassadors are going to represent their nations in State coaches covered with crape!

ALL

'Rah!

EVEREST

And as for princes and dukes and archbishops and such, we're just suffocated with them!

(*Enter* DUTCHY *in spick and span new college-corps costume—black crape scarf on arm.*)

FERGUSON

Hello, what's the matter with you?

WIDOW

Why, poor boy! what is it? are you sick?

(*They help him to a chair.*)

There, now—tell us about it.

DUTCHY

Well, I cot such a fright. But I'm over it now.

(Impressively.)

It was after midnight in Notre Dame—nearly time for day-break and it was my turn to watch in dot little jappel where the remains is. Und it was all still, und I peep out droo de curtain und dere was dot huge cavern of a church stretching out dim wid a spark of a candle here, und a spark of a candle way off yonder; und de soldiers of de guard of honor had dey heads down on de pew-backs all soun' asleep—und so I dought it was all safe, und den I begun.

EVEREST

Begun what?

DUTCHY

Vell I dell you. I lif' de end o'our coffin de very first day she arrive und I say to myself, "It won't do; dey ain't bricks enough in dot coffin."

EVEREST

Boys, he's right. I noticed that, too. Forgot about it.

WIDOW

(Not pleased.)

Lads, it was very careless—we could have got into serious trouble by that. Go on.

DUTCHY

So I had fetched some more bricks done up in a cloak, und a screw-driver; und I got dem out, now und put dem in und yoost got de lid screwed on again when a breest come, und most catch me wid de screw-driver in my hand.

ALL

Great Scott!

DUTCHY

But dot ain't de worst.

CHICAGO

(Absently.)

Cheer up, the worst—

DUTCHY

De breest say de King coming wid de other Kings und Sultans und Emperors to look at de remains.

ALL

Great Christmas!

DUTCHY

De King say he *must* pay dot honor to de mos' illustrious artist since Raffy-*ell*. I told de breest we all afraid de remains ton't *keep* und dot is why we have not allowed de people to see de corpse. But I say if de *King* want to come it's all right—he is very welcome.

WIDOW

You unspeakable idiot!

ALL

Lordy!

DUTCHY

(Undisturbed.)

So I ask de breest what time it is—my watch is stopped—which is a lie. Vell, he ton't know; und I ask him will he be so kind und slip out front und find out. Vell, I always pring a little small lunch there, nights; und I peep out, und when de breest is half way down through de church I snake off de lid und lay my lunch inside de coffin und screw it on again, und bore some little holes over it wid a gimlet.

(Pause.)

EVEREST

Well? − − −What good did that do?

DUTCHY

(Placidly.)

Two pound − − Limburger cheese.

WIDOW

Let me hug you!

ALL

And I.

DUTCHY

I make up my mind it ain't safe for me to leave there till de King come. So when the Spaniard und the Hindoo come, one by one in their turn, I send them away und say I am not tired, I stand the watch myself. Und so, Gott zy Dank, it come out all righd, und we *safe* poys, we *safe*—but I am yoost dead for starvation and no sleep.

(Drops head back and snores a little.)

ALL *(Shake him.)*

CHICAGO

Thunder and blazes, wake up and *finish!*

WIDOW

Did the King come?

DUTCHY

(Sleepily.)

Never come till one hour ago—the King und the Sultan und the others.

(Pause—nodding.)

CHICAGO

(Shaking him.)

Well?—What did they do?

DUTCHY

Noding.

(Half-snore.)

Dey go — — — righd away!

(Snore.)

ALL

(Shake him.)

Wake up!

(They pull him upright in his chair.)

CHICAGO

(Shouting in his ear.)

What—did—the King—*say?*

DUTCHY

(Dreamily.)

Said — — — we ought to — — — buried him — — — — last summer.

ALL

(With enthusiasm.)

You darling!

(Hug him again.)

WIDOW

Come, you splendid old thing, you shall be feasted and bedded like a prince.

(Exit WIDOW *and* DUTCHY.*)*

GORGEOUS FLUNKEY

(Announces the ENGLISH MERCHANT, *the* AMERICAN *and the* AUSTRALIAN *by their names. They enter—in sober black, and shake hands with the* BOYS.*)*

ENGLISH MERCHANT

We have called, on our way to the funeral, to leave our respects for Madame Tillou, and ask after her health.

CHICAGO

She is quite prostrated, which is but natural. I thank you for your courtesy, gentlemen, on her behalf.

(A distant deep bell, tolling.)

AUSTRALIAN

Ah, that sound!

AMERICAN

It notifies the world of a mighty loss.

ENGLISH MERCHANT

Ah, yes, quite irreparable.

(A distant gun.)

AUSTRALIAN

Hear ――― that is the moan of a desolate world.

AMERICAN

The result of the great auction-sale of his pictures must make that stricken poor lady feel very proud.

CHICAGO

(Aside to the BOYS.*)*

Let on that you haven't heard of it!

(*Aloud.*)

The result? The news has not yet reached us.

(*Gun.*)

GORGEOUS FLUNKEY

(*Bringing vast envelope on a salver.*)

For Madame! Condolences — — from his Royal Majesty the King.

(*All bow.*)

(*Exit* FLUNKEY.)

AUSTRALIAN

It was amazing.

AMERICAN

I had an agent there. The Angelus was knocked down to me at 500,000 francs.

CHICAGO, FERGUSON AND O'SHAUGHNESSY

Congratulations!

(*Gun.*)

AMERICAN

(*Sadly.*)

Spare me that, gentlemen. The French government interposed and forced me to give up my bargain for an extra 50,000.

(*Gun.*)

O'SHAUGHNESSY

Ah, it wasn't fair, sir.

GORGEOUS FLUNKEY

(Salver.)

For Madame! Condolences — — — his Royal Majesty the King of Bavaria!

(Gun.)

(Exit FLUNKEY.*)*

(They bow.)

ENGLISHMAN

To think—I had that picture, once, for 2500 francs.

EVEREST

But you listened to Monsieur André — — — it was a mistake. I thought so, at the time.

(Gun.)

FERGUSON

A body couldn't buy the yellow-pine easel it was painted on for that, now.

AUSTRALIAN

I've been offered 300,000 francs for my Sowers.

ENGLISHMAN

You were born lucky, I think. But I got the imitation Angelus, anyway. I'm thankful for that.

THE BOYS

(Aside.)

That's news, anyway.

ENGLISHMAN

Got it for 5,000 francs.

AMERICAN

Of the 27 pictures we left hanging on the walls that day—

ENGLISHMAN

Like a set of idiots—

AMERICAN

Only 3 sold for less than 15,000 francs apiece.

GORGEOUS FLUNKEY

For Madame! Condolences—his Imperial

   (Gun.)

Majesty the Sultan of Turkey!   *(Exit.)*

AUSTRALIAN

The 27 and the Angelus together netted a little over 3,000,000 francs.

O'SHAUGHNESSY

   (Privately to FERGUSON.*)*

And he's painted a million-worth since—hey, Sandy?

FERGUSON

Yes, and he'll go on and paint a million-worth a year.

O'SHAUGHNESSY

Yes, indeedy, for thirty years.

FERGUSON

And we'll dribble them out—one or two a year—and keep up the price.

GORGEOUS FLUNKEY

For Madame! Condolences −−− his Imperial Majesty the Autocrat of all
the Russias!

   (Gun.)

(The distant bell tolls again.)

AUSTRALIAN

There—we ought to be moving, gentlemen.

ENGLISHMAN

Quite right.

(The VISITORS *shake hands.)*

CHICAGO

(Touches bell. A FLUNKEY *appears.)*

(To FLUNKEY.*)*

Show the gentlemen out.

(VISITORS *and* FLUNKEY *exit.*)

(Distant bray of mournful music.)

FERGUSON

(At window.)

Come here, boys! Look at that—ain't it grand! The King!

(It has grown dark.)

O'SHAUGHNESSY

Sultan!

EVEREST

His Majesty of Bavaria!

CHICAGO

Emperor of Russia! Well, a night funeral *is* the most impressive thing in the world!

Just as far as you can see—

(Enter WIDOW.*)*

FERGUSON

Bishops, princes, infantry, cavalry, artillery—

O'SHAUGHNESSY

And all in that splendid glare of light! It'll be two hours passing.

CHICAGO

Rush!—here's your funeral, and it's just a stunner! Look at that! Don't it make you feel good?

EVEREST

And we've selected your new name for you.

WIDOW

What is it?

EVEREST

Placide Duval.

WIDOW

Good.

FERGUSON

You're a rich amateur. Understand?

CHICAGO

Marvelously successful imitator of the late lamented.

WIDOW

Imitator of myself?

CHICAGO

That's it. And you are already getting famous. Our old customers have been here.

EVEREST

My Englishman has bought your imitation of the Angelus. For 5,000 francs.

WIDOW

That is horrible. He bought the *original*, and will never know it. The *other* was the copy.

CHICAGO

That's all right. It's good enough. Worth the money it brought.

WIDOW

(Sorrowfully.)

Ah, boys, I never thought of this. You've killed me for good. Ah. To live maybe fifty years, and suffer the daily torture of that bastard fame—successful imitator of my own works!

CHICAGO

Come—oh, don't. Let's dance it off. Cheer up — — the worst is yet to come.

(They ALL *dance the can-can—distant guns—tolling bells—bray of passing bands, playing mournful music.)*

MARIE

(Appears—amazed.)

(Aside.)

Shameful! — — — Her own brother's funeral! — — — *He* would not act like that.

(Exit.)

Stop, boys. Marie has seen us. I've hurt her—I am ashamed. Go. I must talk with her.

(They start away.)

Chicago, did you get those theatrical things for me?

CHICAGO

Yes, your page has them, and I've posted him—he knows just what to do.

(Exit all but WIDOW.*)*

WIDOW

*(Strikes bell twice—*PAGE *in buttons appears.)*

Ask Mamselle Marie to come here.

PAGE

Yes, Madame. *(Exit.)*

WIDOW

(Solus.)

Poor little abused thing! And I've got to let her come to the wake—no way to get around it. – – Confound those harum-scarum young rascals, they *must* have a wake,—wake *after* the funeral. Got to have everything complete. If they *could* only let on to be sorrowful—but dear me, they couldn't keep *that* up—all rich, now, and full of youth and gay spirits. Those poor old people – – – what will they think, – – – – Placide Duval – – – rich amateur – – –

(Snapping fingers.)

'George, I've got it! – – – I shan't have to disappear from the world at all—shan't even have to leave Paris!

(Enter MARIE, *down cast—*WIDOW *goes and puts arm around her waist—brings her to sofa. Distant music.)*

WIDOW

There, darling, put it on my shoulder. You've been crying again.

(Guns—boom—boom—boom.)

MARIE

Oh, Daisy, how *could* you act so?

WIDOW

Poor dear, it was not my natural self. When I am grieved, I—I am so emotional, you know.

MARIE

(Cheered.)

Oh,—then it was only hysterics.

(Gun.)

WIDOW

That was it.

MARIE

(Kiss.)

Poor dear Daisy! It must be so hard for you. And the others—did they have hysterics too?

WIDOW

Yes, all.

MARIE

How dear and good! I just love them; don't you, Daisy?

WIDOW

Oh, yes, and pity them so!

(Mournful music passing by. Distant guns.)

(Pause—listening.)

MARIE

Oh, isn't it awful! And to think that that is *his* funeral—and we shall never see him again.

(Sobs.)

WIDOW

(Aside.)

Damn it. I feel like an assassin!

(All through the following few speeches, distant music, bells and guns.)

(Aloud.)

Ah, dear heart, how beautiful it would be if this were all a delusion, a dream, and he not dead—this only a *fictitious* François Millet.

MARIE

O, what a sweet thought! Let us imagine it. Go on, darling.

WIDOW

It *is* a pretty thought. Imagine him appearing before you disguised—

MARIE

Oh, how lovely!

WIDOW

And should say his name was—er—now what should his name be?

MARIE

You pick it out, dear!

Well, let me see—Lefevre,—Lafarge—Le—oh, how would Placide do?—
Placide Duval?

MARIE

Oh, that's the one. Placide Duval—I think it's ever so nice. Go on, sister.

WIDOW

And then he would ask you to marry him, you know, and—

MARIE

I'd do it—right away!

WIDOW

Yes, but you forget, you little muggins—his *voice* would be disguised, too.
You wouldn't know him. Even if he *told* you, you mightn't believe him.
And there wouldn't be any way or any sign by which—

MARIE

Oh, yes, there would, yes there would. The pink scar above his wrist—I'll
show you the place.

WIDOW

(Preventing the exposure.)

Oh, yes, I forgot that.

MARIE

Why, we all know that scar.

(Pause—sadly.)

But oh, he is gone, he is gone, and we shall never see him any more. Oh,
Daisy, I'm *sorry* you had that beautiful thought—I shan't ever get it out of
my mind any more, now, and it will break my heart.

(Pause.)

(Solemn boom of distant guns, or music or bells, which have been silent for a while. She rises sobbing.)

O-o-o! hear that!

(Totters away—assisted—passing the window, glances out.)

Returning! He is in the ground! O-o-o, take me away, take me away!

(Crying hard.)

WIDOW

(Aside.)

It breaks my heart!

(Exit BOTH.*)*

(Enter ANDRÉ, *stealthily.)*

ANDRÉ

(Walks about soliloquising—gazing at pictures, busts and things.)

– – – 'George, she's just *rancid* with money. – – Laws, if I hadn't been afraid of that forged contract, I wouldn't give a rap to marry her or *any*body. – – – However, I'll take her if she doesn't go back on me – – I wonder if she will? I believe she'll give me the promise. Yet she's terribly capricious, and uncertain. Chicago—I don't take much stock in Chicago, for all he says he studied for the ministry – – –*he* swears she'll say yes, this time—

(Looking up at a picture—stands where WIDOW *can't see him when she enters.)*

(Enter WIDOW.*)*

(She is entirely bald, black patch over one eye, has a slovenly old peignoir on, which conceals her dress; face is yellow; has a hand mirror; walks on crutches.)

WIDOW

(Solus.)

The dear fellow, he ought to be here in half an hour, I think.

(ANDRÉ *sees her and steps out of range and stares.*)

I've loved him—oh, for a whole month, now.

(*Seats herself at a center-table.*)

There's no resisting him, he admires me so. I couldn't help teasing him. But I think maybe I have worried him long enough, poor darling. Ah, he will be so happy. I must make myself supremely beautiful for him.

(*Strikes bell twice.*)

ANDRÉ

(*Aside.*)

Talk about the ruins of ancient Rome! – – – I wish I—I wish—I suppose there is no way to get out of here without her seeing me.

(*Enter* PAGE.)

WIDOW

Bring my new teeth.

(*Exit* PAGE.)

(*She fusses at mouth.*)

I do think this is the most troublesome set I've ever had. When I *want* to remove them I can't do it, and every time I go to a ball and get excited I cough them out.

ANDRÉ

(*Aside.*)

God bless my soul.

(PAGE *brings the new set on a salver. From behind a screen?*)

(*To be acted—not spoken. Except remark to* PAGE?)

WIDOW

(Puts them in—works mouth.)

They don't fit very well. Take up an awful sight of room. However they are more stylish than the others.

(To PAGE.*)*

Bring me a fresh glass eye—*clean* one.

ANDRÉ

(Aside.)

It's perfectly odious!

PAGE

Any particular one, Madam?

WIDOW

Well, yes—my Sunday one.

(Exit PAGE.*)*

(Fussing at patched eye.)

This troublesome thing — — — it's stuck.

(To be acted—not spoken,—except "It's stuck.")

ANDRÉ

(Aside.)

Oh, my goodness!

WIDOW

Sho! I've turned it with the gilded side to the front.

(Hand-glass.)

Why, it looks like a torch.

(Works at it.)

There—now it's right.

ANDRÉ

(Aside.)

Lord, it's ghastly!

(PAGE brings eye on salver.)

WIDOW

(Holding the eye up and examining.)

Ah, that's a love!

ANDRÉ

(Aside.)

Think of it—she would do that every night before she went to bed. A body couldn't stand it. It would give him night-mare.

WIDOW

There—

(Examines it.)

troublesome thing—I shan't try to wear it again. Dear André, he shall have it for a love-gift.

ANDRÉ

(Aside.)

Not if I know myself.

WIDOW

(Removes patch. Makes winks in the glass.)

This one's all right. Fits snug as a plug. Full of expression, too.

(To PAGE.)

Fetch my hair.

(Exit PAGE.)

Now let me see. Yes—I'll put on the new complexion, now. It'll need time to dry before he comes.

(Turns her back and wipes off the yellow.)

There

(Hand-glass—)

why, it's the loveliest I've ever bought.

ANDRÉ

(Aside.)

Upon my word, I always thought it was natural.

*(*PAGE *brings hair.)*

*(*WIDOW *begins to put it on.)*

WIDOW

Fetch me some legs.

(Exit PAGE.)

ANDRÉ

Isn't any *part* of her genuine?

WIDOW

(Examining wig in glass.)

Dear me, I believe I've injured this, cutting off that lock. But no matter, he begged for it *so* hard.

ANDRÉ

(Aside.)

And so I did.

(PAGE *brings several handsome artificial legs up to knee, stockinged and gartered, on a tray.*)

WIDOW

(*Holding one up.*)

Ah, that's the new American one—and it's a daisy, too.

(*Turns her back*—PAGE *on his knees, helping screw-on leg.*)

Sho', you are all wrong—the heel's in *front.* Turn it around. No—it belongs on the *other* leg.

ANDRÉ

(*Aside—slowly shaking his head.*)

Nothing solid *about* her.

WIDOW

(*Examining legs.*)

They are all *lefts.* Get some more.

(*Exit* PAGE.)

(WIDOW*'s back still turned.*)

ANDRÉ

(*Aside—fervently.*)

I wouldn't marry that débris if she was worth a billion. I'm going to get out or die.

(*Sneaks out.*)

WIDOW

(*Removing peignoir.*)

He's disposed of, I reckon. Ah, the boys missed that circus.

(*Looking at watch and calling off.*)

Come—carry out this rubbish—quick! Time for the wake to begin.

(PAGE *removes the legs and things.*)

(*Distant guns, bells and music.*)

WIDOW

(*Listening.*)

Ah, those poor bricks are at rest.

(*The entire dramatis personae, sweet-hearts and everybody—except* ANDRÉ— *come filing solemnly in, announced, name by name, by a* SPLENDID FLUNKEY (*the servants always have a crape scarf on arm*) *and take their seats.* WIDOW *sits on sofa with head bowed, handkerchief to eyes, when they arrive. The* MEN *salute with a bow in passing, the* OLD LADIES *and* CECILE *silently kiss her forehead.* MARIE *sits down by her* MOTHER.)

MADAME AUDRIENNE

(*To* MADAME BATHILDE.)

Bless us, she's not in mourning!

MADAME BATHILDE

How strange.

(*Beckons to* CHICAGO; *he comes.*)

Why isn't she in mourning?

CHICAGO

She's nearly wild with grief. She can't bear the thought of it. Please don't seem to notice it. Whisper it around—tell the others.

MESDAMES AUDRIENNE AND BATHILDE

Ah, poor thing!

(*The whisper goes from mouth to mouth, answered by satisfied nods.*)

(Strikes bell. FLUNKEY *appears.)*

You and the other servants may retire for the night—all but the concièrge—and he must deny madame to all visitors.

(Exit FLUNKEY.*)*

Does anyone desire to say a few words in memory of our lamented friend?

PAPA LEROUX

(Rises.)

He—he—

(Can't control his voice—solemn silence—women put handkerchiefs to their eyes.)

He—was to me as a son—

MOTHER LEROUX

(Sobbing.)

And would have *been* our son.

MARIE

(Sobbing.)

Oh, it's *so* hard.

PAPA LEROUX

Would have been our son—and that is true. I knew him so long — — — and he was so good and dear — — —

(Sobs all over the house.)

— — — through all his poverty he—he—he shared his farthings — — and his scant food — — — with his young artist friends here — — — oh, those were noble generosities, to come from his poor purse, poor lad, poor lad, poor departed friend of us all — — — and the moment he got rich, that splendid day, that day which was such a strange and beautiful surprise to us all, how he made us all rich!

(Sobs everywhere.)

—how he poured out his money—oh, like water, like water — — — — and saved me, who was ruined—

MOTHER LEROUX

(Sob.)

Ah, that he did, God bless the dear memory of him!

PAPA LEROUX

And there sits my poor child—no comfort for her in this—this—this life any more—

MARIE

(Crying.)

Don't! don't, father!

WIDOW

(Aside.)

I can't stand it!

(Aloud rising.)

Dear friends—good friends—of my poor lost brother—remain where you are, but let me go—I cannot bear these beautiful words, they wring my heart.

MANY

Ah, poor thing, poor thing!

WIDOW

You will let me say good-bye, and God bless you all—we shall meet no more. I go back to my country home and my desolate life. To-morrow a rich stranger will occupy this grand house—with his young wife—a good man and kind, but a recluse—a man with a secret sorrow gnawing at his heart—he thought he was born to fame, but knows he must die unknown. You will know him. Be good to him. He goes disguised—pretend not to notice it.

(MARIE *looks up wistfully.*)

He bears a fictitious name—Placide Duval—

(MARIE *rises, gazing.*)

—Keep his secret. And so, good-bye dear friends. And let me, also leave with you a secret. Swear to keep it thirty days—after that, tell it if you choose—nobody will believe you.

(*All hold up hands.* MARIE *moving dazed and slowly toward him.*)

When France has committed herself to the expression of a belief, she will die a hundred thousand deaths rather than confess she has been in the wrong.

(*Holding up arm.*)

Do you know that scar?

MARIE

François!

(*Embrace.*)

(*Put this fearful music in, or leave it out; either will do.*)

(CHICAGO—*Standing, with arm about* CECILE's *waist—conducting orchestra.*)

CHICAGO

Now!—Ready! The grand International Musical Mosaic!

(*Artists and pupils and several musicians from the theater orchestra snatch out instruments that have been concealed under the chairs, and begin to play, with zeal—but only the orchestra men play* tunes—*and each a* different *tune—a bugle (Marseillaise Hymn); a fife (Yankee Doodle); violoncello or bass viol*

(God save the Queen); hand-organ (Die Wacht am Rhein). Curtain slowly descending.)

Curtain (Music ceases.)

Curtain lifted, a moment.

Tableau.

(DUTCHY *pays, one at a time, 5-franc pieces into* CHICAGO's *hand.)*

DUTCHY

There—

Curtain.

AFTERWORD

MARK TWAIN AND THE THEATRE

Mark Twain was fascinated by the theatre all his life—as an avid theatergoer, as a drama critic, as a close friend of actors and theatrical producers, as a sometime actor in family entertainments, as a writer of works others dramatized for the stage, and as a playwright himself.[1]

During his childhood in Hannibal, Missouri, young Sam Clemens was exposed to mock Shakespearean orations and swordfights, minstrel shows, and amateur theatricals. When he left home at age seventeen, he attended his first professional theatre in New York, Philadelphia, St. Louis, and Keokuk, Iowa. He wrote his sister that he was particularly moved by a Broadway performance by Edwin Forrest in *The Gladiator* in October 1853. By 1856 he had read enough drama criticism in the press to write a hilarious parody of it in one of his more memorable early experiments as a satirist.[2]

Virginia City, Nevada, where Twain lived in the early 1860s, had several flourishing theatres in which touring companies performed mainly romantic and burlesque comedies and farces, and in 1863 the Virginia City Opera House, a theatre as elegant as any in San Francisco, opened its doors. The Virginia City newspaper on which Twain worked, the *Territorial Enterprise*, devoted so much space to its theatre coverage that the Opera House routinely reserved a section of front row seats for *Enterprise* reporters. Twain and his pals on the *Enterprise*, Joe Goodman and Dan De Quille, would attend a play together, each write his own review, have late-night debates about their various reactions, and then decide what to publish—often an amalgam of their responses. Twain claimed that the *Enterprise* quickly became "the best dramatic review on the coast." In San Francisco, where he worked as a reporter in the mid-1860s, surrounded by actors and aspiring playwrights, Twain hoped to earn an extra $40 a month writing theatre reviews for the *Dramatic Chronicle*, an irreverent and satirical publication that became so successful it dropped the word "Dramatic" from its name in 1869, becoming the *Daily Morning Chronicle* (now known as the *San Francisco Chronicle*, it is a major metropolitan daily newspaper). The runaway success of a burlesque by Twain's friend Charles Henry Webb at the San Francisco Academy of Music opened Twain's eyes to the moneymaking potential of the theatre.[3]

Twain would continue to write dramatic criticism—both parodic and serious—throughout his life, and he would continue to attend plays for his own pleasure, in New York, London, Vienna, and elsewhere. He avidly participated in plays privately performed for family and friends. He was an impassioned defender of actors and the acting profession, a close friend of many professional theatre people, and a founding member of The Players, a club in New York.[4] And he persistently tried to make it as a playwright. He succeeded once, spectacularly—and fairly early in his career, at that. But he could never make it happen again.

In 1873, within a month of finishing their collaborative novel, *The Gilded Age*, Twain and Charles Dudley Warner filed a synopsis of "The Gilded Age: A Drama" with the Copyright Office and approached the prominent playwright Dion Boucicault about making a play out of their novel—only to balk at Boucicault's insistence on a third of the profits.[5] Twain and Warner shelved the idea of dramatizing the book for the moment.[6] But in April 1874, they found out that an unauthorized dramatization of *The Gilded Age* starring comic actor John T. Raymond was about to be staged in San Francisco by G. B. Densmore, co-owner and drama critic of the San Francisco *Golden Era*, a literary weekly to which Twain had contributed. Twain soon learned that only the parts he had contributed to the book, and none by Warner, featured in the play and that Densmore's production was "a one-character play" like comic actor Joe Jefferson's famous performance as Rip Van Winkle in a play by Dion Boucicault (a role in which Jefferson starred almost continuously from 1866 until 1904). The one fresh character showcased in the production was Twain's irrepressible Colonel Sellers. Twain proposed to Warner that they split their copyright, each retaining dramatic rights to the characters he alone had created. Warner agreed, Densmore was persuaded to close his pirate production, and Twain set to work on his own version of the play. He finished it in a month, leaving in little of Densmore's language but keeping much of his plot.[7]

Actor John Raymond, who had appeared in the short-lived, unauthorized San Francisco production, played the title role of Colonel Sellers when the play opened at the Park Theatre in New York on September 16, 1874, after some tryout performances in upstate New York. The role made Raymond's career. Twain never thought much of *Colonel Sellers* as a play ("It is simply a setting for the one character, Col. Sellers, and as a *play* I guess it will not bear a critical assault in force," he wrote William Dean Howells), and he was never happy with how Raymond interpreted the role. But it was hard to argue with success. The indefatigable Colonel Sellers's determination to make his fortune in steamboats or mules or hogs or congressional appropriations or liniment for sore eyes gave the phrase "There's millions in it!" to American popular culture. The play would become one of the biggest hits of the decade, and at one point would bring Twain more annual income than all of his books combined.[8]

George Odell's *Annals of the New York Stage* dubbed *Colonel Sellers* "a wretched thing," while the *New York Tribune* called it "excessively thin in texture." However, the play's one original character, the upbeat and self-assured speculator Colonel Sellers, managed to offset the play's weak dialogue and insipid romance plot and win over even the most impatient critics. Even a critic like Brander Matthews, who found the plot "arbitrary and weak and unconvincing," had to admit that Colonel Sellers, the embodiment of Americans' "ingenious inventiveness and our incurable optimism," was enormously appealing. Seven months after the play opened in New York, Twain bragged to his brother-in-law Charlie Langdon that "in Brooklyn, Baltimore, Washington, Cincinnati, St. Louis & Chicago, the play paid me an average of nine hundred dollars a week. In smaller towns the average is $400 to $500." And that was only Twain's half of the earnings; the other half went to Raymond. For the rest of Twain's life the memory of the fortune that *Colonel Sellers* had brought him would regularly lure him back into writing for the stage.[9]

Of his next effort as a playwright—*Ah Sin*, a collaboration with Bret Harte—the less said, the better. *Colonel Sellers* may have been "a wretched thing," but at least it made money. *Ah Sin* was even more wretched and was also a financial flop. The play exploited "the Heathen Chinee" from Harte's popular poem

"Plain Language from Truthful James" and built on Harte's moderately successful popular drama *Two Men of Sandy Bar*. Harte came to Hartford in the fall and winter of 1876 to write the play with Twain. Before they were done personal animosities between the two would explode into a bitter feud that would last the rest of their lives. The comedy-melodrama they wrote is so embarrassingly bad that it is tempting to attribute as little of it as possible to Twain. Twain himself claimed that Harte wrote it while Twain played billiards, with Twain later going "over it to get the dialect right." That may overstate the case, but perhaps not by too much. The play opened in Washington, D.C., at the National Theater on May 7, 1877, and closed within a week. When Augustin Daly moved it to New York a critic from the *Sun* wrote that "As a piece of dramatic work the play is beneath criticism." On opening night in New York, Twain gave a speech after the play, which struck the audience as infinitely more amusing than the comedy that had just been performed. Twain told them that the more Daly had cut, "the better the play got. I never saw a play that was so much improved by being cut down; and I believe it would have been one of the very best plays in the world if his strength had held out so that he could cut the whole of it." John Raymond, who had starred in *Colonel Sellers*, called *Ah Sin* "the worst play he ever saw." Twain himself took to calling it "that dreadful play."[10]

Twain succeeded in getting only one other play he wrote professionally produced—if a one-night stand by an elocutionist can, indeed, be considered a "production." His 1883 play, *Colonel Sellers as a Scientist*, was, like *Ah Sin*, an ill-fated collaboration, this time with his friend William Dean Howells. As the title suggests, it was an effort to spin off a sequel to his profitable earlier venture by featuring the same character that made the first play a success. But it was not to be. The play was filled with gimmicks, beginning with the flame-throwing "fire-extinguisher" that accompanied Colonel Sellers's entrance. But actor John Raymond, who had brought Colonel Sellers to life in the earlier play, refused to have anything to do with this one because he and Twain had come to dislike each other intensely and because he felt the play was weak. And because Raymond was so closely associated with the role, no other actor of any standing would touch it. Howells eventually turned over his rights in the play to Twain, and after settling financially with theatrical manager Daniel Frohman (who had rented the New York Lyceum to Twain before it had become clear that the play was unlikely to succeed), Twain leased the theatrical rights to an elocutionist and impersonator named A. P. Burbank. After a try-out in New Brunswick, New Jersey, in September 1884, the play opened and closed in New York on the same day.[11]

Although others managed to successfully adapt *The Prince and the Pauper, Pudd'nhead Wilson*, and *Tom Sawyer* for the stage during Twain's lifetime, *Colonel Sellers, Ah Sin*, and *Colonel Sellers as a Scientist* were the only plays Twain wrote himself that were professionally produced.[12] Nonetheless Twain per-colated with real and hypothetical dramatic projects from the 1860s on, ex-perimenting with dramatic sketches, fragments, one-acts, and occasionally, longer plays as well. Some were burlesques or travesties that helped Twain hone his skills as a parodist—such as send-ups he wrote of *Hamlet* and *Il Trova-tore*, and his rather leaden burlesque of Alan Pinkerton's detective stories, *Cap'n Simon Wheeler, the Amateur Detective*. There was his bilingual playlet *Meisterschaft*, written for a German-conversation class made up of his friends; a fragment about a hard-working, hard-drinking reporter involved in a love triangle *(Beau Brummel and Arabella)*; notes for a play about the Franco-Ger-man war of 1870–1871; and a one-act melodrama about Oliver Cromwell *(The Death Wafer)*. Twain came up with other bright ideas, as well: "Speak to How-ells about Dramatizing Don [Quixote]," he jotted in his journal. Twain and Howells also discussed the possibilities of collaborating on an abolition spy drama and a play set in the Sandwich Islands. "If we should ever let ourselves loose on the drama we could write a pile of plays," Howells effused; over the years, Howells and Twain each published prolifically, but nothing came of these projected collaborations. And for the most part, the forays into theatre that Twain did make before 1898 are best remembered—when they are worth remembering at all—as rough drafts and notes for work that would take shape more successfully in other genres (for example, Twain eventually trans-formed the ill-fated play *Colonel Sellers as a Scientist* into his last comic novel, *The American Claimant).*[13]

Twain had been tantalized and frustrated by the theatre world all his life. But during his first winter in Vienna in 1897–1898, that world pulled him into its orbit with a force greater than any he had encountered before.[14] Sur-rounded by a broad range of superb productions in spectacular state-of-the-art theatres and courted as a collaborator by one of Austria's leading play-wrights, Twain couldn't resist the siren call of the stage. He jumped into a frenzy of projects—translating plays that were hits on the Viennese stage for

Mark Twain at the Hotel Metropole
in Vienna. Courtesy Mark Twain
Papers, The Bancroft Library.

production in the United States, collaborating with Viennese playwright Siegmund Schlesinger on a series of plays about contemporary social issues, and writing a new comedy of his own. All that is known to survive from this flurry of activity is one work: *Is He Dead?*

Theatre was central to the cultural life of fin-de-siècle Vienna. Stefan Zweig observed that "the first glance of the average Viennese into his morning paper was not at the events in parliament, or world affairs, but at the repertoire of the theater, which assumed so important a role in public life as hardly was possible in any other city."[15] The city's dozen or so major resident repertory companies would present as many as seventy-five different works in a given season, characterized generally by extremely high standards of performance and productions that spared no expense. Twain's excellent German allowed him to take full advantage of the city's rich theatrical offerings. He attended plays constantly and also cultivated the theatres' managers, directors, and leading actors.

The manager of the Burgtheater, Max Burkhardt, gave Twain a private V.I.P. tour of the theatre in October 1897, just after Twain recovered from gout. Carl Dolmetsch tells us that the theatre's new electric lights were turned up in the house for his visit (a favor usually reserved for visiting royalty) and the stage crew gave him a private demonstration of the theatre's machinery for special effects, said to be the most advanced in Europe. At the end of the tour, Dolmetsch writes, Twain "asserted unequivocally that the Burgtheater was *das schönste Theater der Welt* (the most beautiful theater in the world) and the tour itself 'worth the trouble of a trip to Vienna.'"[16] The Burg's repertoire, during Twain's stay in Vienna, included plays by Friedrich von Schiller, Johann Wolfgang von Goethe, and Gotthold Lessing, along with excellent German translations of William Shakespeare (*Richard II, A Midsummer Night's Dream*), and a fresh hit from Paris, Edmond Rostand's new play, *Cyrano de Bergerac*. Twain returned again and again to a play by Adolf von Willbrandt, *Der Meister von Palmyra* (The master of Palmyra), a play that argued that endless life would mean endless suffering (Twain so admired the play—which he called "one long, soulful, sardonic laugh at human life"—that he published an article in an American magazine chastising his countrymen for not demanding more plays like it on Broadway).[17] The vitality of the theatre world Twain encountered in Vienna helped fire his ambition to write for the stage again, as did his conversations with Austrian playwright Siegmund Schlesinger.

In January 1898, Schlesinger, an experienced dramatist who had had over fifteen comedies and tragedies produced, proposed that he and Twain collaborate on a play entitled *Der Gegenkandidat, oder die Frauen Politiker* (The opposing candidate, or women politicians). The play was particularly timely since there was increasing agitation in Austria in the 1890s—as there was in the United States, England, and elsewhere in Europe—for women's political rights. Twain supported Rosa Mayreder, the Susan B. Anthony of Vienna, and gave a reading while in Vienna for the pro-suffrage organization Mayreder had founded, the Allgemeiner Oestereichischer Frauenverein (General Austrian Women's Association). Twain was delighted with the progress he and Schlesinger had made on their play by early February. They also outlined a play they planned to write together entitled *Die Goldgräberin* (The woman gold-miner) that was to star Emperor Franz Josef's mistress, Kati Schratt—also topical, given the 1897 discovery of gold on Klondike Creek in the Yukon that was widely covered in the Viennese press (Twain and Schlesinger called off the gold-miner play after an unpleasant meeting with Schratt herself).[18] Neither of Twain's collaborations with Schlesinger was completed, and no fragments of their work together are extant. But it is worth noting that at the same time that Twain was writing *Is He Dead?*—a play that features a highly unusual "woman" character—he was also working on plays that involved women characters in unconventional roles.

Twain was also excited about the idea of translating Viennese hits into English, acquiring the American and English rights to them, and mounting them in London or New York. During the spring of 1898, he translated *Bartel Turaser*, a naturalistic drama by Czech-born Philipp Langemann that premiered in Vienna in December 1897. (The play was about a starving worker who accepts money to cover up his boss's sexual assault of a female fellow-worker and who is then ostracized by the community and hounded by his guilty conscience.) Twain also translated *Im Fegefeuer* (In purgatory), a farce by Ernst Gettke and Alexander Engel, who were known for their light comedies and operettas; it was about young lovers circumventing parental disapproval. Twain then interested himself in translating Theodor Herzl's play *Das neue Ghetto* (The new ghetto), a play about the rise of anti-Semitism in Austria that Twain had seen during its premiere at the Carl-Theater on January 5, 1898.[19] As Twain hobnobbed with the successful actors, directors, and playwrights who helped put on the stunningly diverse array of impressive plays that made Vienna's theatre scene so vibrant, Twain found himself determined, once again, to try to write a popular play of his own.

Soon after entering in his notebook the date "New Year's, 1898," Twain wrote "'Is He Dead?' Millet the painter." The next entry in the journal reads: "Play-denouement. Girl to recognize disguised sweetheart by a false note in a song which they had formerly used as a signal."[20] On January 14, 1898, he wrote, "Began to write comedy 'Is he Dead?' (François Millet)." Twain finished it by February 5.[21]

What was this famous philistine doing writing a play about art? And why did he fix on the French painter Jean-François Millet as its central character? As it turns out, Twain had been writing about art in a range of complex ways far longer than is often recognized, and it was almost overdetermined that this particular artist, more than any other, should have become the focus of his attention.

MARK TWAIN AND ART

Twain's comments on art in his first travel book, *The Innocents Abroad* (1869), earned him the reputation of a philistine who rarely missed a chance to discredit the Old Masters. In time, however, Twain developed a sincere appreciation for art and counted many artists among his close friends; he would even bankroll the Paris apprenticeships of two American artists.

Typical of the kind of remark that earned Twain the reputation of being hostile to art is his comment, after being traipsed past innumerable buildings designed by Michelangelo, "I never felt so fervently thankful, so soothed, so tranquil, so filled with a blessed peace, as I did yesterday when I learned that Michael Angelo was dead."[22] This remark is, in part, Twain's exhaustion speaking, as well as his response to the guides' demand that the tourists genuflect at every mention of the great artist's name. Elsewhere in the book Twain voices at least a penumbral understanding of the many factors that can shape a person's response to a work of art, admitting that if he saw each painting in the Vatican in a room by itself, as he saw Raphael's *Transfiguration*, he might take a more positive view of it.

Twain's most memorable comments on art in *The Innocents Abroad*, however, connect the spirit of the work of art and the attitude of the artist to the conditions under which the art was produced. In the Louvre, Twain tells us, he looked at

> miles and miles of paintings by the old masters. Some of them were beautiful, but at the same time they carried such evidences about them of the cringing spirit of those great men that we found small pleasure in examining them. Their nauseous adulation of princely patrons was more prominent to me and chained my attention more surely than the charms of color and expression which are claimed to be in the pictures.[23]

Twain's critique here of the system of princely patronage that produced so many of the Louvre's paintings is consistent with his efforts throughout this book to debunk the obligatory reverence his fellow Americans felt compelled to show before the icons of European culture. But the fact that this argument fit Twain's political agenda does not mean that Twain did not believe it. He did feel that the cozy relationship between so many Old Masters and the corrupt social system in which they painted detracted from the value of the art they produced. Part of the appeal of Jean-François Millet to Twain undoubtedly would stem from the fact that Millet was not the beneficiary of innumerable commissions from barons and princes and that his most sublime paintings portrayed ordinary laborers, not wealthy patrons. In Millet's paintings, in place of the "nauseous adulation of princely patrons," one finds respect for the common man and the common woman—a sensibility whose politics were infused with the spirit of democracy.

Twain preferred his own discoveries in art to the received wisdom of the guidebooks. During a trip to London in 1874, he spent most of a day looking at paintings of animals by popular British painter Edwin Henry Landseer, mounted after his death in a large exhibition at the Royal Academy. Many of the pictures were on loan for the first time from Queen Victoria's private collection. Twain found them "wonderfully beautiful," in large part because of their uncanny realism ("if the room were darkened ever so little & a motionless living animal placed beside a painted one, no man could tell which was which").[24]

Twain's most extended published comments on art next appear in *A Tramp Abroad* (1880). When Twain returned to the galleries of Europe twelve years after his first visit, he found that he "had learned one thing"—that the originals were superior to the copies, contrary to his initial views on this subject.[25] But, in fact, he had learned a good deal more. *A Tramp Abroad* is filled with Twain's meditations on what constitutes greatness in art. He quotes with guarded approval a local artist who opined that, although the Old Masters "often drew badly" and "did not care much for truth and exactness in minor details," "there is a *something* about their pictures which is divine—a something which is above and beyond the art of any epoch since. . . . "[26] This same sense of the ineffable quality of truly great art—the "*something* . . . which is divine"—would pervade Dutchy's and Chicago's conversations about Millet's painting *The Angelus* in *Is He Dead?*

Twain's ability to appreciate art increased during the twelve years since his first trip to Europe—although the pleasure he found "in contemplating the Old Masters" was still "a calm pleasure; there was nothing over-heated about it."[27] Lawrence Oliver has observed that in general, Twain's "taste in the fine arts was governed by the same basic principles that governed his taste in literature: put simply, he admired art that could appeal to common people, [and] that was a sincere expression of the artist's vision and emotions . . . [H]e scorned the esoteric, sensational, idealized, and slavishly imitative."[28] He also had no patience for the effusions of art critics and made fun of their language whenever the opportunity presented itself. Of a forty-foot canvas by one of the Bassano family of Italian painters, Twain writes, "Some of the effects are very daring, approaching even to the boldest flights of the rococo, the sirocco,

Mark Twain sitting for a sculpture portrait by Theresa Fedorowna Ries in December 1897 in the artist's atelier in Vienna. The Russian sculptor's alabaster bust was exhibited that season at the Kunstlerhaus. For more about Ries see her book, *Die Sprache des Steines* (Vienna: Krystall, 1928); she writes about working on Twain's bust on pp. 26–27. Photograph by Scolik Picture Archives of the Austrian National Library, Vienna.

and the Byzantine schools. . . . "[29] Twain also parodied art criticism in "Instructions in Art," a two-part article he published in the *New Metropolitan* in April and May of 1903. The piece included ten of his own rudimentary sketches, including a cartoon of a naked woman leaping into the air in unalloyed exuberance. Twain titled this crude figure sketch "JOY. Symbolical work" and had this to say about it:

> The present example is an impressionist picture, done in distemper, with a chiaroscuro motif modified by monochromatic technique, so as to secure tenderness of feeling and spirituality of expression. At a first glance it would seem to be a Botticelli, but it is not that, it is only a humble imitation of that great master of longness and slimness and limbfulness. . . . That thing in the right hand is not a skillet, it is a tambourine.[30]

Twain enjoyed poking fun at art critics, tour guides, and travelers who mouthed received opinions of works of art instead of looking at them with their own eyes. Nonetheless, it would be a mistake to assume that he didn't take art and artists seriously, for he did. He sponsored apprenticeships in Paris for two artists from Hartford, his Connecticut hometown. The first was a white sculptor named Karl Gerhardt, whose bust of Twain appears on the frontispiece of the first American edition of the *Adventures of Huckleberry Finn*.[31] The second was a black painter named Charles Ethan Porter, who absorbed lessons from Barbizon School painters during his sojourn in France, and whose Barbizon-influenced paintings were well received on his return to the United States.[32] Twain was close friends with the painter Francis (or, Frank) Millet from the time he executed a famous portrait of Twain in 1876. (Frank Millet, an American who pronounced his name like the words "kill it," was no relation to the French painter with whom he shared a last name.) Other artist friends included Robert Reid and Edward Simmons, with whom Twain spent time during stays in New York City, and Frederick Church, whom he visited at Church's estate near Hudson, New York. And artists, including Ignace Spiridon (who painted portraits of Twain and his daughter Clara the year he wrote *Is He Dead?*), frequented the lively gatherings Twain hosted at the Hotel Metropole in Vienna.[33]

Despite the objections to patronage that he raised in his first travel book, Twain was frequently a patron of the arts himself. And despite his characteristic irreverence and refusal to kowtow to received opinions about art,

Twain's respect for artists shone through in the friendships he formed with them throughout his life.

WHY MILLET?

From the 1870s through the 1890s, Americans were obsessed with the French painter Jean-François Millet—so much so that they earned a reputation in England for being "Millet-mad," as one contemporary observer put it.[34] Given the massive interest his countrymen had in this painter, Twain may well have believed that from a purely commercial standpoint, a play about Millet was destined to be a hit.

It began with a handful of American art students who went to the village of Barbizon, southeast of Paris, at mid-century to study with Millet and then returned to the United States championing his genius and persuading wealthy Bostonians to collect his work. These young men were both passionate and articulate about art, and many of them wrote articles about their mentor in prominent American newspapers and magazines. They found the pathos of the myth of the starving, neglected artist that became enshrined in the American imagination during the quarter century after Millet's death appealing (if not totally accurate) and helped feed the media's infatuation with the artist and his work. The intense bidding war that broke out between France and America in 1889 over *The Angelus*—and that painting's subsequent exhibition across the United States—made it the most famous painting in the world by the century's end. All of these factors left their mark on *Is He Dead?*

Born to a modestly successful peasant family in the village of Gruchy, near Cherbourg, in Normandy in 1814, Jean-François Millet showed an early talent for art. His family sent him to Cherbourg to study with local painters, and the city of Cherbourg sent him to Paris for further training, where he studied briefly in the studio of history painter Paul Delaroche. Millet's first submission to the Salon exhibition, in 1839, was rejected, but the following year one of two portraits he submitted was accepted. He married in 1842 but his young wife died two years later. He remarried and struggled to earn a living by painting portraits, biblical subjects, and scenes drawn from mythology. In 1848, with the exhibition of *The Winnower* at the Salon, Millet attracted attention for the scenes of peasant life for which he would eventually become renowned. He sold the painting for 500 francs to the French minister of the interior, who also gave him a state commission.

Jean-François Millet, 1856–1858. Nadar [pseud. of Gaspard Félix
Tournachon] (photographer). Salt. 26.3 × 19.6 cm (10¹¹/₃₂ × 7¾ in.).
The J. Paul Getty Museum, Los Angeles. Copyright © The J. Paul Getty
Museum.

When a cholera epidemic broke out in Paris in 1849, Millet moved his family to a three-room cottage in the village of Barbizon, on the outskirts of the
forest of Fontainebleu, where he would live for most of the rest of his life, a
town already home to other artists including his good friend Théodore
Rousseau. A detached barn-like structure built a few years later opposite the
house became Millet's studio. From 1850 on, he concentrated on the rural
themes for which he would be best known (drawing images both from scenes
around him in Barbizon and from his memories of rural life during his Nor-

Jean-François Millet. *The Sower.* 1850. Oil on canvas. 101.6 × 82.6 cm (40 × 32½ in.). Museum of Fine Arts, Boston. Gift of Quincy Adams Shaw through Quincy Adams Shaw, Jr. and Mrs. Marian Shaw Haughton. 17.1485. Copyright © 2003 Museum of Fine Arts, Boston.

mandy childhood). In 1860 Millet bound himself to give virtually all of his annual output to a dealer in exchange for a monthly stipend. The peak of the fame Millet would earn during his lifetime came at the Paris Exposition of 1867. But not long after that, his health declined. He died in 1875. Twelve years after his death, France gave him a major retrospective exhibit.

Seventeenth-century Flemish painters may have depicted peasants at work, but Millet's peasants had a rough dignity and courage unlike any that had appeared before. Was his exhausted *Man with a Hoe* a statement about the plight of impoverished agricultural workers? Was his forceful, striding *Sower* meant to convey those workers' potential strength and power?[35] Millet denied that he had any political agenda and always claimed that his preoccupation was with aesthetics and not ideology, that he was just painting life as he saw it. Although many members of the French bourgeoisie of his day recoiled from the spectre of social insurrection his work suggested to them, many young artists found his respect for ordinary people and the challenges of their hard lives revelatory.

In the United States, his reputation steadily climbed due to the parade of American art students, artists, and collectors who had been finding their way to Barbizon since mid-century, connecting Millet with American markets. One of Millet's earliest American protégés was William Perkins Babcock, who arrived in Barbizon from Boston in 1848 and stayed until after Millet's death. Babcock became a close friend and introduced Millet to many of his fellow Bostonians. A second protégé, William Morris Hunt, who went to Barbizon in 1851, helped introduce Millet and other Barbizon School painters to Boston collectors such as Quincy Adams Shaw, who acquired scores of Millet's oil paintings and pastels. Hunt went on to become Boston's most respected artist, as well as a very popular teacher and writer on art.[36] Another protégé was Edward Wheelwright, who would become the art editor of the *Atlantic Monthly* in the 1870s, during William Dean Howells's tenure as editor there. Wheelwright's lengthy article on Millet in 1876 did much to set the tone for the cult of Millet that flourished in the United States from the 1870s through the 1890s. Two of Millet's final protégés were Wyatt Eaton and Will Hicock Low, both of whom would publish prominent articles about Millet— Eaton in the *Century Magazine* in May 1889 and Low in *McClure's Magazine* in May 1896. From early on, as Susan Fleming observes, "it became a must for Bostonians visiting Paris to journey to Barbizon to meet Millet, whether or not they were able to buy his paintings." By 1889, thirty different collectors in Boston owned Millets.[37]

Although a handful of collectors outside of Boston (such as New York's August Belmont, Baltimore's William T. Walters, Philadelphia's Adolph E. Borie, and Henry Probasco of Cincinnati) had acquired Millets in the 1850s, 1860s, and 1870s, Millet's popularity in the rest of the country peaked in the 1880s and 1890s.[38] In 1893, when the protagonist in Howells's novel *The Coast of Bohemia* commented that "if the right fellow ever came to work, he could

Jean-François Millet. *The Gleaners*. 1857. Oil on canvas, 83.6 × 111 cm. Inv.: RF 592. Photo: Jean Schormans. Musée d'Orsay. Copyright © Réunion des Musées Nationaux/Art Resource, NY.

get as much pathos out of our farm folks as Millet got out of his Barbizon peasants," Howells felt no need to explain his allusion.[39] By this time Millet's renown stretched from coast to coast, with California collector Charles Crocker owning works including *Wool Carder* and *Man with a Hoe* (the latter would inspire Edward Markham to write his famous poem by the same title in 1899, shortly after the painting was exhibited in San Francisco). By 1896, many of Millet's greatest paintings were in America, and reproductions of his paintings (such as *The Gleaners*) decorated homes across the country.[40]

To the wealthy American families who avidly collected Millet's art during the last quarter of the nineteenth century, portraits of peasants didn't convey the terrors of revolution that they had to the French bourgeoisie decades earlier. Rather, American industrialists found the paintings' mellow earthtones calming and saw in Millet's weary peasants a nod to the nobility of the everyman idealized by American democracy. Hunt had supplied Millet with

French translations of Ralph Waldo Emerson, who proclaimed, "I embrace the common . . . and sit at the feet of the familiar and the low" and who challenged anyone to "dare claim that a potato is inferior to a pomegranate."[41] We do not know Millet's response to Emerson's work, but we do know the respect he had for the image of the humble potato, which figures prominently in his paintings. A nation that had been exhorted by the Transcendentalists to value "the familiar and the low" was primed to appreciate Millet's achievement in art.

None of Twain's contemporaries drew comparisons between Mark Twain's work and the art of Millet (although they did compare Millet's achievement in painting with Walt Whitman's in poetry, as did Whitman himself).[42] That is not surprising, since Twain's work was still relatively new and undigested, its larger significance often missed until the twentieth century. But looking back on these two towering figures in the arts today, a parallel is striking: both men made great art out of subjects that their predecessors had viewed as too ignorant or too poor or simply too unimportant to be worth delineating in paint or in print—including French peasants, American slaves, and the poorest of poor whites. Twain and Millet were, in this respect, kindred spirits—a fact which may help explain the sincerity and passion that inform the appreciation of Millet conveyed in *Is He Dead?*

Twain precedes the play with a note acknowledging that he has "taken the pardonable liberty to highly antedate" (by almost half a century) the bidding wars over Millet's *Angelus* that occurred after Millet's death. But there are other apparent departures from the historical record as well, including the central love plot; the international, multiethnic crew of artists; Twain's characterization of Millet's relationship with his agent/art-dealer; and Twain's depiction of the degree of poverty and neglect that Millet suffered.

By the time Millet settled in Barbizon, he was thirty-five years old, married, and the father of three children. Six more children would be added shortly thereafter to the household of this devoted family man and patriarch. In the play, however, Twain makes him "about 25" and single, resembling not so much the historical Millet as the many would-be suitors who swarmed around Twain's very eligible twenty-three-year-old daughter Clara in Vienna, creating an atmosphere that Clara's teacher waggishly dubbed "Delirium Clemens."[43] While the historical Millet had nine children, Twain's Millet has nine artist friends and pupils who function, in some ways, as dependents. The historical Millet, like Twain's protagonist, was surrounded by aspiring artists and students, but none of the accounts of life at Barbizon suggest a group quite as diverse and international as the one that surrounds Millet in the play. However, Twain's cast of French, American, German, English, Irish, Scottish, Indian, Chinese, Turkish, and Spanish artists may well reflect the visitors "of many nations and ranks" who congregated in Twain's apartments at the Hotel Metropole while he was writing the play.[44]

The art students who came to Millet for guidance did not all paint in Millet's studio. They usually took rooms elsewhere in the town and brought their work to his studio for comments; he would view their paintings on one of the several easels he kept set up in his studio for this purpose. But Twain's description of Millet's studio (the stage set for acts 1 and 2 of *Is He Dead?*) as lofty and spacious, with a sofa, several backless chairs and a tall easel, accurately reflects aspects of a detailed description that appeared in the *Atlantic Monthly* in 1876, as well as a line drawing from a photo of Millet's studio that appeared in the *Century Magazine* in 1889.[45]

Although it is true that Millet signed over to an agent all of the work he produced during a period of time in exchange for a sum of money, their relationship was characterized by none of the exploitation and dishonesty represented in the play. In fact, the real agent/art-dealer, Alfred Sensier, was one of Millet's closest friends and most devoted supporters, as well as his dedicated biographer. If there was a real-life model for the villainous André, his identity is unknown. It is perhaps worth noting, however, that this is the play Twain wrote at the moment that he emerged from the clutches of creditors who had driven him into bankruptcy. Perhaps some of the acrimony he felt during this period toward various "villains" in his own life found its way into his characterization of the avaricious André.[46]

One of the most striking departures from the historical record would appear to be Twain's exaggeration of Millet's poverty and desperation, and of the obscurity and neglect he suffered during his lifetime. The historical Millet was generally not starving and suicidal, and France had recognized his talent on at least a few occasions with prizes, commissions, and inclusion in prestigious exhibits.[47] As it turns out, on this subject, at least, Twain was simply repeating the distortions first promulgated by Sensier's 1881 biography, which put forth the idea that Millet was desperately poor and shamefully neglected by his country. Sensier was so effective at articulating this idea, and other writers were so willing to accept it, that the "Millet myth" became firmly entrenched in the American imagination.

Twain maintains fidelity to the growing consensus in the United States in the 1890s about Millet's character as a man and talent as an artist, in the words of Sensier, "a painter who gives life to the humble, a poet who exalts ignored splendours, a good man who encourages and consoles."[48] Millet was known for being kind, generous, intelligent, warm-hearted, and underappreciated during his lifetime; and he was respected for having painted resonant, powerful, and moving works of "noble simplicity"—"no fuss, no feathers, no tricks of color, no theatricals," as Chicago puts it in the play. In *The Angelus*, Chicago sees "just that solemn half-light, and those brooding distances for the chimes to wander through, and those two humble figures, so poor outside, so rich with the peace of God in their hearts. Dutchy I'd rather be the painter of that picture than — — — look here, that picture's going to make a strike to-day—you'll see." By the time Twain wrote those words, that painting *had* made "a strike"—and not just any strike: *The Angelus* had sold for more than any painting in history, inaugurating the age of the extravagant art auction of the modern era. Twain knew that viewers of the play would be aware of this fact; he could assume that the dramatic irony would add to the play's appeal.

Twain might have seen *The Angelus* when he attended the Paris Exposition of 1867 on the trip that he immortalized in *The Innocents Abroad*, since it was displayed there along with *The Gleaners* and seven other paintings by Millet.[49] Or he might have seen it when the painting toured the United States in 1889, attracting crowds in cities across the country. In any case, he could not have missed the massive number of lengthy profiles of the man who painted it that appeared from the mid-1870s through the 1890s in journals and newspapers Twain read and contributed to—such as the *Atlantic Monthly, Century Magazine, Harper's,* and *New York Times*—articles that would have familiarized Twain with the details of Millet's life. In addition, the publisher of the first English translation of Sensier's biography of Millet in the United States was also Twain's publisher at the time—and Twain's friend and traveling companion. Twain must have relished the fact that Americans had generally appreciated Millet's gifts earlier, and with more enthusiasm, than the French had—a fact that gave him a welcome opportunity to feel superior to tastemakers in Paris.

Millet's obituaries in American newspapers in 1875 "set the national

Jean-François Millet. *The Angelus*. 1857–1859. Oil on canvas. Photo: C. Jean. Musée d'Orsay. Copyright © Réunion des Musées Nationaux/Art Resource, N.Y.

mood for our perception of Millet's life as fraught with incessant and futile struggles for survival and recognition," as Laura Meixner has observed, preparing the way for Sensier's full-blown version of this story several years later. The *New York Times*, for example, reprinted a *Pall Mall Gazette* account that misunderstood the unpretentiousness and simplicity of French rural funeral rites and launched into a screed against France's shameful neglect of the great painter: "Our great painter has passed away in his poverty, unnoticed in the desolation of indifference. . . . No one spoke a word of commemoration over the dead. Poor Millet leaves a widow and nine children, no fortune, [and] a studio full of unfinished works . . . which will make the fortunes of twenty picture dealers."[50] Three months after Millet's death, the Boston Athenaeum's exhibit of the Quincy Adams Shaw collection prompted heated debates in American newspapers and periodicals about Millet's style, which continued into the fall of 1875, when the *Atlantic Monthly* weighed in with its own editorial on the subject.[51]

The lengthiest major article about Millet in the American media after the flurry of obituary attention in 1875 appeared in the *Atlantic Monthly* in September 1876: "Personal Recollections of Jean-François Millet" by Edward Wheelwright, art editor of the *Atlantic Monthly* who had gone to Barbizon in 1855 to become Millet's student. The article included memories of the "animated and noisy" conversation among the many young artists in the town, as well as detailed descriptions of Millet's atelier—complete with "piles of canvases, new and old, of all sizes; many of them . . . pictures in various stages of progress," "several . . . easels," and a "calico-covered couch"—all looking rather "untidy and neglected."[52] We know that Twain read a piece by his close friend, William Dean Howells, the magazine's editor, in the same issue of the *Atlantic Monthly* and, given how closely Twain tended to read that publication, it is highly likely that he was familiar with Wheelwright's article, as well.[53]

In 1880, an English translation by Helena De Kay of Alfred Sensier's biography of Millet was serialized in *Scribner's Monthly Magazine*. The following year, De Kay's translation of Sensier's biography was published in book form and reviewed prominently in the national media. The book's publisher was James R. Osgood, who would bring out *The Prince and the Pauper* in 1881 as well, and who in early 1882 would be Twain's traveling companion on a steamboat trip down the Mississippi.[54] Laura Meixner observes that "the legend, as fabricated by Sensier, exaggerated the facts of Millet's biography, focusing upon egregious overstatements of his hardships which won the artist widespread public sympathy." Although twentieth-century critics, most notably Robert Herbert, have endeavored to revise and rectify Sensier's exaggerations and misstatements, it was the myth promoted by Sensier and others that fascinated Americans—and that clearly intrigued Mark Twain. Meixner writes that "woven throughout the narrative biography, graphic descriptions of the travail Millet suffered at the hands of his creditors inspired within readers a sympathetic and charitable response."[55] Typical, for example, is this passage from Sensier:

> Millet had around him a group of tradesman, anxious and almost fierce, whom he had to appease. A baker, the only one in the place, threatened with oaths to withdraw the daily bread. A grocer had become his bailiff. A country tailor . . .

sent the sheriff's office to seize the furniture in his studio, and he would not allow the artist a day's or even an hour's grace. Such scenes were repeated over and over during many years.[56]

As a result of taking scenes like these as "the literal fact of Millet's biographies," Meixner writes, "Americans came to view his life as one of unrelieved persecution and the artist himself as a martyr bravely resigned to abject poverty"—which was precisely the response Sensier had hoped for, believing that an awareness of the obstacles Millet had faced "ought to raise him in our esteem."[57] By "embellishing accounts of Millet's self-denial, courage, religious faith, and sense of duty, Sensier conferred upon him the attributes of a hero. These qualities, coupled with his peasant heritage, made Millet an ideal example for a democratic nation founded on agrarian origins. Both the myth and the myth-maker, then, were immediately embraced by the American public," reinforced by writers and lecturers who extolled, in articles, lectures, and even poems the legendary virtues of "an unsung heroic figure who had borne a life of unrelieved hardship with dignity."[58]

Throughout the 1880s, Millet's former students continually published reminiscences of Millet in prominent magazines Twain read. For example, Twain is likely to have seen the article on Millet by Wyatt Eaton that ran in *Century Magazine* in 1889, since Twain frequently contributed articles to *Century Magazine* and read it regularly. Eaton's article included a line drawing (based on a photograph by Karl Bodmer) of Millet's studio.[59] Other articles about Millet from the 1880s that Twain may have seen appeared in the *Atlantic Monthly*, the *Nation*, the *New York Times*, and the *New York Tribune.*[60]

A lengthy profile in a British publication that Twain sometimes read took the occasion of the 1888 Millet exhibition at the École des Beaux-Arts to reiterate the Millet myth first laid out by Sensier, replete with the "hungry days and sleepless nights, . . . cruel attacks and cold neglect which embittered his whole existence. . . . " The author of the article, Mrs. Ady (who, under the name Julia Cartwright, would bring out an updated version of Sensier's biography in English in 1896) also noted that the strains of "constant work and worry" led Millet more than once to consider suicide—a point he reaches in *Is He Dead?* before Chicago comes to the rescue.[61]

But the attention the American press had paid to Millet during the 1870s and 1880s was dwarfed by the barrage of articles that appeared in the summer of 1889, when *The Angelus* was the subject of an unprecedented international bidding war. Millet had painted *The Angelus* between 1857 and 1859, commissioned by Thomas Gold Appleton of Boston (an acquaintance of Twain's friend William Dean Howells), who neglected to claim the painting after it was finished.[62] During the next thirty years, it had changed hands a number of times, owned variously by French and Belgian collectors. The prices of Millet's paintings soared after his death in 1875. *The Angelus*, which Millet had originally sold for 1,800 francs, had been purchased by Belgian collector John W. Wilson for 38,000 francs in 1873, and was bought by M. E. Secrétan for 160,000 francs in 1881, who sold it for 200,000 francs, and then bought it back himself for 300,000 francs. The painting had also captured the interest of wealthy American industrialists and art collectors Cornelius Vanderbilt and John D. Rockefeller, each of whom bid on the picture unsuccessfully at various times.[63]

On July 1, 1889, M. E. Secrétan put *The Angelus* up for sale in the first art auction to resemble auctions held today, complete with an illustrated advance catalogue and a fair measure of hoopla in the press. A fierce competition broke out between A. Proust, who represented the French government, and James Sutton, who represented the American Art Association. "Nothing can describe the frenzy, the emotional passion of the hour," one observer wrote in the *New York Times*. Proust placed the winning bid: 553,000 francs, an astronomical price for a painting (in a lead story and headline on page one the next day, the *New York Times* translated the purchase price as $111,000). But when the French government refused to authorize the expenditure, the sale was made to the American. Sutton allowed the painting to be exhibited in France for two days before beginning its journey to the United States, where the American Art Association planned to exhibit it around the country.[64]

In the United States, *The Angelus*'s reputation preceded it: the sensational bidding war made instant celebrities of the painting and the artist who had painted it. On October 15, 1889, the *New York Times* reported that "the highest-priced picture of modern times" had arrived in New York on the steamer *La Bourgogne*. The newspaper went on to say that applications to exhibit Millet's painting had already been received from St. Louis, Washington, D.C., Philadelphia, Boston, and Chicago, and that those cities would have the first opportunities to show it. The painting enjoyed an unprecedented notoriety due both to the stories about the sale that had flooded the nation's press and to the enterprise of the individuals who exhibited it around the country, charging admission to every viewer. As the "Editor's Easy Chair" column in *Harper's* in April 1890 noted, "There was never so costly a picture as the 'Angelus' of Millet exhibited in this country. The throng of spectators was incessant. A procession of pilgrims was constantly ascending the stairs. . . ." The picture, "which was carried up in the bidding at the sale in Paris to such a price that the news was dispersed through Christendom the next morning," was one of the "topics of daily talk." The editor was uncertain as to whether the long procession of visitors who lined up to see the picture was more like a parade of "devotees to a shrine" or a "crowd [lined up to see] a circus."[65]

The adventures of *The Angelus* helped spark a new wave of articles about Millet in the 1890s. There were two articles in *Scribner's* in 1890, and in 1891 and 1892, there were at least six articles about Millet in the *New York Times*. *Century Magazine* ran a long piece on Millet by his brother in January 1893, and Twain himself published his short story about Millet, "Is He Living or Is He Dead?" in *Cosmopolitan Magazine* in September of that year (that short story is discussed in the following section). *Century Magazine* published another biographical article by Millet's brother in April 1894, and in 1895 the *Saturday Review of Politics, Literature, Science and Art* ran an evaluation of Millet's achievement in art. The publication of Julia Cartwright's biography of Millet in 1896 (an adaptation and expansion of Sensier's earlier work) provided the impetus for yet another round of Millet stories in the press. Cartwright's book was reviewed in the *New York Times, Westminster Review, Living Age, Dublin Review, Dial, Citizen, Athenaeum*, and elsewhere, between 1896 and 1897. In 1896 there was a profile of Millet in *McClure's Magazine* by one of his protégés, Will Hicock Low (which contained full-page or half-page reproductions of *The Angelus, The Gleaners*, and nine other paintings by Millet, as well as a full-page image of his studio, from a photograph by Karl Bodmer). An article on "Millet and Whitman" ran in the *Atlantic Monthly* in 1897.[66]

When Twain wrote *Is He Dead?* he surely planned to capitalize on Millet's name recognition and reputation as he tried, one last time, to craft a hit play. Yet the sincerity and passion with which Dutchy and Chicago discuss the beauty of *The Angelus* suggests that, at the same time, Twain himself may have been genuinely moved by Millet's painting. He may have been attracted to it because it embodied aesthetic values he endorsed, and he may have admired it for many of the same reasons so many of his countrymen did. But an addi-

Millet's studio as it was depicted in *Scribner's Magazine* 7, no. 5 (May 1890): 59. According to the original caption, the illustration was made "from a photograph by Charles [Karl] Bodmer, made three months after the artist's death, precisely as he left it, except that the color stand near the easel had been moved."

tional hypothesis for his attraction to it is suggested by an interpretation of the painting put forward decades after Twain's death by surrealist painter Salvador Dalí. In his strange and quirky book *Le Mythe Tragique de L'Angelus de Millet*, Dalí writes that he found *The Angelus* "the most troubling of pictorial works, the most enigmatic, the most dense, the richest in unconscious thought that had ever existed." Dalí claims to have surveyed all of Western art and failed to find another painting with precisely this configuration of two people—a placement of figures that puzzled and disturbed him. He developed a theory about the back-story of the scene represented on the canvas and managed to persuade the Louvre to x-ray the painting to allow him to test his hypothesis. When the results came back, Dalí announced that they provided the evidence to support his theory. What the x-ray revealed, in the painting's foreground, under the basket of potatoes, was part of an oddly shaped geometric form that Millet had painted over. Dalí saw that shape as the possible outline of a small coffin. The scene of afternoon prayer in the field, then, may be also a scene of mourning—for the couple's dead child.[67] Given that in the winter of 1897–1898, Twain himself had only just begun to emerge from the grim period of mourning for his own lost child, the subdued, elegiac aspect of *The Angelus* may have spoken to his condition, if only on a subliminal level. This reading of the picture resonates at least in part with Millet's own description of his purpose. Although Catholic tradition defines the "Angelus" prayer as commemorating the mystery of the Incarnation, Millet's grandmother, and Millet himself, thought of it as a prayer in which the living recall those who have passed on. As Millet put it in a letter in 1865, "The Angelus is a painting which I did while thinking how, while at work in the fields, my grandmother never failed to respond to the bells, to stop us at our work, and make us say the prayer of the Angelus for the poor dead, piously, hat in hand."[68]

IS HE DEAD? IN RELATION TO TWAIN'S OTHER WORKS

Twain customarily recycled plots, themes, phrases, even characters' names in his works. *Is He Dead?* is no exception. Twain's own previous writing is the single most important source for this play.

Twain based *Is He Dead?* directly and quite explicitly on a short story he'd written five years earlier, which appeared in *Cosmopolitan Magazine* in September 1893 (and was reprinted in *The Man That Corrupted Hadleyburg and Other Stories and Essays* in 1900). "Is He Living or Is He Dead?" is centered on a tale supposedly told to the unnamed narrator by a man he calls "Smith" ("partially to disguise him") during the narrator's stay at a remote resort on the French Riviera in 1892. This short story represents Twain's first effort to work through the ideas that will come together in much more effective form in *Is He Dead?*

One evening, after consuming his second hot scotch in front of a cozy fire in the parlor of his hotel suite, "Smith" tells the narrator a story he has kept secret for many years. When he and his friends were poor and struggling young artists, they hit rock-bottom in a Breton village, and a then-unknown fellow artist named François Millet, who was as poor as they were, took them in and kept them from starving. The four "became fast friends, doting friends, inseparables. We painted away together with all our might, piling up stock, piling up stock, but very seldom getting rid of it." Finally the creditors refused them credit for another centime, and they realized their circumstances were desperate. Millet got to the point of wishing that "somebody would come along and offer us a cabbage" for his painting *The Angelus*. Then one of the group came up with a plan to make them rich, based on the same principle that animates Chicago's plan in the play—"This law: that the merit of *every* great unknown and neglected artist must and will be recognized, and his pictures climb to high prices after his death."[69]

But the scheme is presented in outline form only and not fleshed out with the kind of details that make the play live and breathe. The story *tells*, while the play *shows*. In the story, Millet was disguised as his own distant relative, and even helped carry his own coffin; but he went disguised as a nondescript male relative with none of the Widow's charm. There was no Marie and no André; no love interest or love triangle; no Chicago and no Dutchy; no bumbling journalists and no solicitous neighbors; no Chimney Sweep art critic; no virtue rewarded and villainy punished; no state funeral; no sly crack at the expense of those French citizens who refused to be dissuaded from the belief that Alfred Dreyfus was guilty. Most important, perhaps, there was almost no dialogue.[70] Twain had the basic idea that would blossom into *Is He Dead?* five years later, but he had not yet found the right genre for it.

Twain's story, however, had adventures of its own in Japan, where one of the country's leading early twentieth-century authors, Takeo Arishima, decided in 1922 that it contained the germ of a good play, unaware that Twain had reached the same conclusion nearly a quarter century earlier. "Is He Living or Is He Dead?" was the first work of Mark Twain's to be translated into Japanese. The story was published in a Japanese magazine in November 1893, two months after Twain published it in *Cosmopolitan Magazine* and decades before Japanese translations of *Tom Sawyer* and *Huckleberry Finn* would appear.[71] Arishima, a member of the influential Shirikaba school of Japanese humanists, wrote a play loosely based on the story, but featuring starving Japanese artists instead of Barbizon-School followers of Millet. Arishima made one of the same changes that Twain had when reshaping the story for the stage: he added a love interest for Domomata, the Millet figure in Arishima's play.[72] While Twain's play has not been available in print until now, Arishima's play, entitled *Domomata no Shi* (The death of Domomata), was published in 1922 in a small-circulation Japanese magazine and was republished the following year in Arishima's collected works.[73] According to Tsuyoshi Ishihara of Otemon Gakuin University in Osaka, Arishima's play is recognized by scholars in Japan as the best-known Japanese literary adaptation of any work by Mark Twain.[74] There are records of the play having been performed twice during Arishima's lifetime (he died in 1923, the year after his play was published); and it is still performed by college drama groups and amateur theatrical ensembles today.[75] Dr. Ishihara is currently translating it into English.

While his short story "Is He Living or Is He Dead?" bears the most direct relation to *Is He Dead?* of all of Twain's earlier fiction, Twain borrowed themes, subjects, styles, and stances from other stories as well. Thematically, Twain's play *Is He Dead?* reprises aspects of "The Legend of the Capitoline Venus," a six-chapter "condensed novel" Twain published in 1869.[76] Each chapter of "The Capitoline Venus" takes place in a setting designated by a bracketed phrase at its start. The setting of chapter 1, for example, is *"[Scene—An Artist's Studio in Rome.]"* The bracketed *"[Scene]"* that begins each chapter, and the dominance, throughout, of dialogue, makes this piece read like a play. A struggling young sculptor named George loves a young lady named Mary, and she loves him; but Mary's father, loathe to let his daughter "marry a hash of love, art, and starvation," requires that George acquire fifty thousand dollars before he will say yes to the wedding. Mary's father gives the suitor six months to raise the money. George despairs of his ability to accumulate that sum, given that when the piece begins he is in arrears for his board. But a boyhood friend named John Smith saves the day. While George looks on, aghast, John takes a hammer and deliberately smashes the nose, fingers, ear, toes, and leg of one of George's sculptures, the figure of a woman he had called "America." John then puts both "the broken-hearted artist and the broken-legged statue" aboard a carriage, leaves the artist at his lodgings, and drives off with the statue without revealing his plan.

The day the stipulated six months are up, George wishes he were dead. When a knock at the door comes, he assumes it is another creditor. Instead, it is a former creditor pressing him to take a gift. And the next knock is Mary's father announcing, to a bewildered but ecstatic George, "My noble boy, she is yours! . . ." All is revealed in the next chapter, set in a Roman café, where a group of American gentlemen read and translate a story in a Roman newspaper that makes clear what has happened. George's friend, John Smith, had bought a small piece of land in the Campagna six months earlier, just beyond the tomb of a wealthy Roman family now fallen on hard times. Smith transferred the title to George, explaining that "he did it as payment and satisfaction for pecuniary damage accidentally done him long since upon" some property belonging to his friend. Then,

> Four weeks ago, while making some necessary excavations upon the property, Signor Smitthe unearthed the most remarkable ancient statue that has ever been added to the opulent art treasures of Rome. It was an exquisite figure of a woman, and though sadly stained by the soil and the mould of ages, no eye can look unmoved upon its ravishing beauty. The nose, the left leg from the knee down, an ear, and also the toes of the right foot and two fingers on one of the hands, were gone, but otherwise, the noble figure was in a remarkable state of preservation.[77]

The government at once took possession of the statue and appointed a commission to assess its value and determine how much to pay the owner of the ground on which it was found. They finally "decided unanimously that the statue is a Venus, and the work of some unknown but sublimely gifted artist of the third century before Christ. They consider it the most faultless work of art the world has any knowledge of." George receives five million francs from the government. The creator of the highly valued art in "The Capitoline Venus" is presumed to be many centuries dead, while the creator of *The Angelus* in *Is He Dead?* is presumed to be recently dead, but in both cases the basic principle is the same: living artists starve while the work of dead artists fetches fortunes. Both works satirize the process by which value is assigned to a work of art.

A number of Twain's other works prefigure aspects of *Is He Dead?* as well. For example, when Chicago asks the Widow whether she's going to Millet's funeral, she responds, "No I'm not. The idea of a man attending his own funeral. I never heard of such a thing." But Twain's readers *had* heard of such a thing—in *The Adventures of Tom Sawyer* (1876)—where attending his own funeral is one of Tom's most memorable adventures, and they would probably have appreciated this playful reference to one of Twain's most famous works. (Twain reprises this imaginative gambit in *Is He Dead?* with enough style to gratify even Tom Sawyer, who surely would have loved to watch all the crowned heads of Europe pay their respects.)

Some of the same lunacy of the Widow's encounter with Mesdames Audrienne, Bathilde, and Caron when they come to pay their condolences in *Is He Dead?* may be found in "An Encounter with an Interviewer," a sketch Twain published in 1874.[78] Exchanges like the following one prefigure the Widow's bizarre responses to the neighbors' questions about her children:

Q. Had you, or have you, any brothers or sisters?

A. Eh! I—I—I think so,—yes,—but I don't remember.

Q. Well, that is the most extraordinary statement I ever heard!

A. Why, what makes you think that?

Q. How could I think otherwise? Why, look here! who is this a picture of on the wall? Is n't that a brother of yours?

A. Oh! yes, yes, yes! Now you remind me of it, that *was* a brother of mine. That's William,—*Bill* we called him. Poor old Bill!

Q. Why? Is he dead, then?

A. Ah, well, I suppose so. We never could tell. There was a great mystery about it.

Q. That is sad, very sad. He disappeared, then?

A. Well, yes, in a sort of general way. We buried him.

Q. *Buried* him! *Buried* him without knowing whether he was dead or not?

A. Oh no! Not that. He was dead enough.

Q. Well, I confess that I can't understand this. If you buried him and you knew he was dead—

A. No! no! we only thought he was.

Q. O, I see! He came to life again?

A. I bet he did n't.

Q. Well, I never heard anything like this. *Somebody* was dead. *Somebody* was buried. Now, where was the mystery?

A. Ah, that 's just it! That 's it exactly. You see we were twins,—defunct and I,—and we got mixed in the bath-tub when we were only two weeks old, and one of us was drowned. But we didn't know which. Some think it was Bill, some think it was me . . . [79]

In *Is He Dead?* the neighbors are as befuddled by the Widow's responses to their questions as the interviewer was to Twain's.

Is He Dead? was not Twain's first tale to involve male cross-dressing. Indeed, male cross-dressing figures in a number of Twain's works. Recall, for example, that Huck Finn, disguised in girl's clothing, is unmasked as a boy—a "runaway 'prentice"—by Mrs. Judith Loftus in *Huckleberry Finn*, when he fails to throw and catch "like a girl." And Tom Driscoll, in *Pudd'nhead Wilson*, dons women's clothing as his disguise when he commits burglaries.[80] Interestingly, during the same year that he wrote *Is He Dead?* Twain found his mind running back to a story he had first jotted down in the 1870s about a household servant named Alice who tripped a burglar alarm to admit her lover and announced (when caught) that the workman had gotten her pregnant in the course of their long affair. Sometime after the narrator pressures the man into marrying her, Alice reveals that she herself was, in fact, a male transvestite.[81] Twain was fascinated by the theatricality of cross-dressing, as Susan Gillman has noted, and had played with the challenges of men performing as credible women before.[82] But never before had Twain explored this topic with the aplomb he demonstrates in *Is He Dead?*

When he takes Millet and several of his friends to the brink of suicide before Chicago devises the clever scheme that saves them, Twain is repeating a plot element he employed in a novel he published four years before he began writing his play *The Tragedy of Pudd'nhead Wilson*. There the slave Roxana decides to commit suicide and murder her child rather than face the prospect of having her child endure the degradations of slavery. She is pushed to the brink—and, indeed, is arranging what she and her child will wear to their deaths—when she comes up with the idea of switching her child's clothes (and fortunes) with those of her master's child.[83] In both *The Tragedy of Pudd'nhead Wilson* and *Is He Dead?* the scam is implicitly justified by the desperation that necessitates it.

Is He Dead? has relatively little in common with Twain's other plays, but a handful of parallels are worth noting. Both *Colonel Sellers* and *Is He Dead?* began in another genre, as prose fiction. Twain wrote each in a matter of weeks, and Colonel Sellers himself is as ebullient and self-confident as Chicago will be.[84] Each act of *Colonel Sellers* ends with the same "Tableaux and Curtain" finish that Twain will employ as his ending to act 3 of *Is He Dead?* But beyond these fairly trivial connections, these two plays are very different from each other. The dialect spoken by the young Chinese art student, Li-Hung-Chang, in *Is He Dead?* is not totally unlike that of the title character in Twain's play *Ah Sin*, but there the parallels with that embarrassing disaster end.

In *Following the Equator*, Twain first explored the conundrum of the "long dog," the dog "like a bench" that is the topic of conversation at the start of act 2 of *Is He Dead?* On the train back from Baroda, India, Twain encountered "a remarkable looking dog":

THE

ATLANTIC MONTHLY:

A MAGAZINE OF LITERATURE, SCIENCE, ART, AND POLITICS.

VOL. XXXVIII.—SEPTEMBER, 1876.—No. CCXXVII.

—◆—

PERSONAL RECOLLECTIONS OF JEAN FRANÇOIS MILLET.

THE recent death of Jean François Millet has suggested the following reminiscences of a period when the writer enjoyed somewhat exceptional opportunities of intercourse with the distinguished French painter; they are largely derived from letters written at the time, supplemented by a still vivid recollection of many circumstances.

I first saw the village of Barbison and made the acquaintance of Millet early in the month of October, 1855. Upon leaving the United States I had been given a letter to him by my friend William M. Hunt, then recently returned from a long residence in France, where for several years he had known Millet intimately. Indeed, the latter told me afterward that "Hunt was the most intimate and best friend he had ever had." I had caught from Mr. Hunt something of his own enthusiasm for the talent and character of his friend, and was anxious to put myself, if possible, under the instruction of one whom he esteemed so highly.

Accordingly, soon after my arrival in Paris, I went down to Barbison, where Millet resided, and — I quote from a letter written at the time — "presently found myself in Millet's *atelier* and in the presence of the great man. I had been told that he was a rough peasant ; but peasant or no peasant, Millet is one of Nature's noblemen. He is a large, strong, deep-chested man, with a full black beard, a gray eye that looks through and through you, and, so far as I could judge during the moment when he took off a broad-brimmed, steeple-crowned straw hat, a high rather than a broad forehead. He made me think at once of Michael Angelo and of Richard Cœur de Lion."

After presenting my letter and answering a few questions about our common friend, I proceeded to the object of my visit, and expressed my desire to become Millet's pupil, or at least to have his advice as to my future course. I had brought with me a few drawings and studies in oil as specimens of my proficiency; these he examined with interest, and criticised courteously but freely. Other visitors now coming in, I took my leave, promising to return after I had taken a stroll about the environs.

Returning to the inn at noon, I found the table set for a *déjeuner à la fourchette*, and I sat down with the other guests, about twenty in number, mostly young men, and all apparently artists. The conversation was animated and noisy. I ate my meal for a while silent and unnoticed, doing my best to understand the jokes every one but myself seemed to enjoy so heartily, but at last I unwittingly attracted the attention of

First page of September 1876 article in the *Atlantic Monthly* by Millet's protégé Edward Wheelwright, art editor of the magazine.

I had not seen one of its kind before, as far as I could remember. . . . It was a long, low dog, with very short, strange legs—legs that curved inboard, something like parentheses turned the wrong way (. Indeed, it was made on the plan of a bench for length and lowness. It seemed to be satisfied, but I thought the plan poor, and structurally weak, on account of the distance between the forward supports and those abaft.[85]

The dog's owner is proud of the dog and shows Twain prizes it won in England and India:

He said that when he walked along in London, people often stopped and looked at the dog. Of course I did not say anything, for I did not want to hurt his feelings, but I could have explained to him that if you take a great long low dog like that and waddle it along the street anywhere in the world and not charge anything, people will stop and look. He was gratified because the dog took prizes. But that was nothing; if I were built like that I could take prizes myself. I wished I knew what kind of a dog it was. . . .[86]

By the time he wrote *Is He Dead?* Twain had discovered that the dog was a dachshund.

In *Is He Dead?* Twain finally figured out what to do with a prop that hadn't quite worked when he tried to use it before: limburger cheese. As it turns out, Twain was not the first writer to extract humor from a case of mistaken identity involving limburger cheese and a corpse. R. Kent Rasmussen tells us that the humorist J. M. Field mined this vein in a sketch published in 1846, and the humorist Artemus Ward did the same in a lecture that Mark Twain heard him give in Nevada in 1863.[87] Mark Twain first wrote his own version of this joke around 1877 in "The Invalid's Story," a piece which his friend William Dean Howells dissuaded him from including in *A Tramp Abroad* (1880), but which he managed to work into the *Stolen White Elephant, Etc.* (1882) and *Merry Tales* (1892).[88] In this slight sketch about a man trying to accompany the coffin of a recently deceased friend on a railway journey (a story which novelist Anne Bernays characterizes as "an anecdote stretched, like a rubber band, until it almost snaps"), Twain has not yet mastered the art of holding back information from the reader.[89] Indeed, the narrator is such a poor storyteller that he ruins all suspense and gives away his punch line near the story's start: "As the train moved off a stranger skipped into the car and set a package of pe-

culiarly mature and capable Limburger cheese on one end of my coffin-box—
I mean my box of guns. That is to say, I know now that it was Limburger cheese,
but at that time I had never heard of the article in my life, and of course was
wholly ignorant of its character."[90] During the two decades that passed before Twain brought out the Limburger cheese again, he had learned a thing
or two about narrative technique that breathed new life into the old gag.

Is He Dead? is also not the first work in which Twain explored the idea of
the "constructed" body. In "Aurelia's Unfortunate Young Man," a bizarre and
macabre little sketch originally published (under the title "Whereas") in 1864,
a young woman's fiancé is so beset by unfortunate accidents that she is faced
with the prospect of furnishing her "mutilated lover" with "wooden arms and
wooden legs, and a glass eye and a wig" before the wedding.[91] In "The Story
of the Old Ram" in chapter 53 of Roughing It (1872), narrator Jim Blaine de-
scribes a "Miss Jefferson" who

> had a glass eye and used to lend it to old Miss Wagner, that hadn't any, to receive
> company in; it warn't big enough, and when Miss Wagner warn't noticing, it
> would get twisted around in the socket, and look up, maybe, or out to one side,
> and every which way, while t' other one was looking as straight ahead as a spy-
> glass. . . . [H]er own eye was sky-blue and the glass one was yaller on the front
> side, so whichever way she turned it it didn't match nohow. . . . When she had
> a quilting, or Dorcas S'iety at her house she gen'ally borrowed Miss Higgins's
> wooden leg to stump around on. . . . She was as bald as a jug, and so she used to
> borrow Miss Jacops's wig—Miss Jacops was the coffin-peddler's wife. . . . [92]

And in "The Lowest Animal" (1897), Twain contrasts the grace and beauty of
the Bengal tiger with "Man—that poor thing," the animal of the wig, the glass
eye, and the wooden leg.[93]

At least two of the characters in Is He Dead? have names that Twain had used
before, or share names with real-life individuals Twain knew, although the
characters in the play bear no relation to these other figures. The Widow Tillou
shares the name of Cornbury S. Tillou, a French miner and jack-of-all trades
whom Twain knew in Nevada in 1861.[94] "Dutchy" is the nickname of a "German lad" Twain recalled from his Hannibal childhood in chapter 54 of Life on
the Mississippi, while Dutchy's last name, "Von Bismarck," comes from that
of German chancellor Otto von Bismarck, whose long-awaited memoirs were
published posthumously the year that Twain wrote Is He Dead?[95]

And Twain took Chicago's signature line in the play verbatim from a letter he had written to his wife the day after he had declared bankruptcy. "Cheer up," he had written Livy, "the worst is yet to come."[96] (Both Twain and Chicago turn out to have been right.)

Finally, it is worth noting that the title Twain chose for this play reprises the punch line of one of the most memorable jokes in *The Innocents Abroad* and extends the implications of that joke. For Europeans, and indeed for most Americans who preceded Twain as travelers to Europe, the proper stance for an American in the face of the grandeur that was Europe was awestruck admiration—a stance Twain rejected at every opportunity. He tells us, for example, that the guide in Genoa "had something which he thought would overcome us":

> "Ah, genteelmen, you come wis me! I show you beautiful, O, magnificent bust Christopher Colombo!—splendid, grand, magnificent!" . . . The doctor put up his eye-glass—procured for such occasions:
>
> "Ah—what did you say this gentleman's name was?"
>
> "Christopher Colombo!—ze great Christopher Colombo!" . . .
>
> "Well, what did *he* do?"
>
> "Discover America!—discover America, Oh, ze devil!"
>
> "Discover America. No—that statement will hardly wash. We are just from America ourselves. We heard nothing about it. Christopher Colombo—pleasant name—is—is he dead?"[97]

The famous "is he dead?" line resonates with the larger trope of European culture as centered on a dead past and American culture as centered on a living present. Twain did not invent the "is he dead?" joke, but he brought it to new heights. "Guides cannot master the subtleties of the American joke," Twain tells us. He celebrated his compatriots' limberness of mind while taking potshots at acolytes of the Old World's ossified artifacts. More than thirty years later, in *Is He Dead?* Twain would return to the idea that Europeans valued the work of dead artists over the work of living ones.

TWAIN AND THE FRENCH

Although Twain is extremely sympathetic to a number of individual French men and women in *Is He Dead?* (including the Leroux family and Jean-

François Millet himself), Twain's familiar antipathy toward the French comes across in the Widow's final speech. After asking all her assembled friends to keep the real identity of "Placide Duval" (a.k.a. Millet, a.k.a. the Widow) secret for thirty days, she tells them that they are free after that to "tell it if you choose" for "nobody will believe you." The reason? "When France has committed herself to the expression of a belief, she will die a hundred thousand deaths rather than confess she has been in the wrong."

Twain's longstanding dislike of the French is probably behind this line, but the most proximate target of this parting shot is undoubtedly the Dreyfus Affair, which gained new prominence in the world press during the weeks when Twain was writing *Is He Dead?* On January 13, 1898, the French writer Émile Zola published in the French newspaper *L'Aurore* his famous *J'Accuse*, an open letter to the President of France; it set off a worldwide furor and was immediately reprinted around the world (in Vienna it was translated into German by Theodor Herzl). Zola's scathing exposé of how French anti-Semitism perverted the cause of justice in the Dreyfus Affair is sometimes referred to as the greatest newspaper article in history. In 1894, an innocent Jewish captain in the French army named Alfred Dreyfus was court-martialed, wrongly convicted of treason, and sentenced to life in prison on Devil's Island off French Guiana. Several years later the real culprit—a Major Ferdinand Esterhazy—was identified. On January 11, 1898, the military mounted a massive cover-up and found Esterhazy innocent. Two days after that Zola (a novelist not previously known for meddling in politics) exploded in righteous rage in his open letter in the pages of *L'Aurore*, charging the government with persecuting Dreyfus out of anti-Semitism. Zola himself was convicted of libel as a result and chose temporary exile in England over jail. Eventually Zola's letter helped bring down a government and helped give Alfred Dreyfus back his freedom, his good name, and his life.

The Dreyfus Affair—and in particular, Zola's role in it—affected Mark Twain deeply.[98] Indeed, at one point Twain planned to write his own book on the subject and was frustrated that his publisher's lack of interest killed the project.[99] Twain, who had been a partisan of Dreyfus since 1896, read *J'Accuse* and became one of its greatest admirers, finding numerous occasions to refer to it and to celebrate its author as a genuine hero.[100] One week after *J'Accuse* was published—on January 20—Twain wrote his friend Henry

Huttleston Rogers that he was putting the "finishing touches" on *Is He Dead?*[101] It is likely that Twain's reading of *J'Accuse*—so fresh in his mind—shaped his pointed choice of Millet's penultimate line in the third act of Twain's play.

In 1899, when exploring an unrelated topic, Twain wrote, "We have none but the evidence for the prosecution, and yet we have rendered the verdict. To my mind, this is irregular. It is un-English; it is un-American; it is French. Without this precedent Dreyfus could not have been condemned." In another piece he wrote around this time, Twain described the execution of an innocent American army officer, despite the evidence in his favor, because "in the end it was found impossible to ignore or get around the French precedent." Most significantly, the Dreyfus case lies at the heart of what may be Twain's most important essay, "My First Lie and How I Got Out of It" (1899), which anatomizes "the lie of silent assertion." "From the beginning of the Dreyfus case to the end of it," Twain wrote, "all France, except a couple of dozen moral paladins, lay under the smother of the silent-assertion lie that no wrong was being done to a persecuted and unoffending man." Twain used the Dreyfus case in this powerful essay as an example of an occasion when the "lie of silent assertion" held sway over a population, "the silent assertion that there wasn't anything going on in which humane and intelligent people were interested." Twain was so moved by *J'Accuse*, that after reading it he wrote, "Ecclesiastical and military courts made up of cowards, hypocrites and time-servers can be bred at the rate of a million a year and have material left over; but it takes five centuries to breed a Joan of Arc and a Zola." Jim Zwick suggests that "Mark Twain's own decision to speak out against U.S. imperialism after his return to the United States in 1900 may have been influenced by his appreciation of Zola's courageous stand during the Dreyfus Affair."[102]

France may have produced a Joan of Arc, an Émile Zola, and a Jean-François Millet, but for Twain, the country's sins outweighed its virtues, and the depravity of the Dreyfus trial was about what Twain had come to expect from a society whose morality (in Twain's view) left much to be desired across the board. In an essay he published in *Harper's* in 1899, when Twain wrote that "I am quite sure that (bar one) I have no race prejudices," the one exception to which he referred was his prejudice against the French.[103]

The seeds of this prejudice, which grew over the course of Twain's career, were planted during his first trip to France in 1867. Twain records his earliest responses to France and the French in 1869 in his first travel book, *The Innocents Abroad*. The dislike that would grow later in his career had not yet set in. Although he was frustrated by the lack of soap in French hotels and by the shave inflicted on him by a Parisian barber, and although "tedious and tiresome" travel in French railway cars made him nostalgic for stage-coaching in the American West, Twain found much to admire. He found everything about the French landscape "charming to the eye," was awed by the beauty of the gardens at Versailles, and enjoyed "rich Burgundian wines" and French food. Twain pokes fun at the arrogant French guides but portrays them as no more impossible than most of the guides he encountered in Italy. One can see signs of things to come, however, in Twain's response to the revealing can-can ("The idea of it," Twain wrote, "is to expose as much of yourself as possible if you are a woman"): he placed his hands over his eyes to avoid seeing it (although he admits to peeping through his fingers). "I supposed French morality is not of the straight-laced description which is shocked at trifles," Twain concluded dryly. Later in the book, Twain ends his retelling of the story of Abelard and Heloise with a condemnation of "the nauseous sentimentality that would enshrine for our loving worship a dastardly seducer like Pierre Abelard."[104] Twain's disapproval of French morality would congeal, as time wore on, into a generalized antipathy toward the French.

Twain's notebooks from the 1870s on, as R. Kent Rasmussen observes, are "filled with invective about the French and their alleged predilections for adultery, prostitution, general immorality and artificiality."[105] Many of these dyspeptic entries date from the cold and damp winter and spring of 1879 when Twain, living in Paris at the time, was trying to finish *A Tramp Abroad* and was suffering from rheumatism and dysentery. Some typical remarks in this vein are his comment that "In certain public indecencies the difference between a dog & a Frenchman is not perceptible"; or "truth, to [a Frenchman], is a thing to be told when it will answer the purpose as well as a lie"; or "A Frenchman's home is where another man's wife is"; or the "French are the connecting link between man & the monkey"; or "France has neither winter nor summer nor morals—apart from these drawbacks it is a fine country."[106]

The failure of the French to get his jokes—and the mess French translators made of them—was another source of irritation that fueled Twain's anti-French prejudice. *Sketches, New and Old*, for example, which Twain published in 1875, includes a hilarious piece entitled "'The Jumping Frog.' In English. Then in French. Then Clawed Back into a Civilized Language Once More By Patient, Unremunerated Toil."[107]

France's failure to appreciate fully the importance of Millet's art until after his death helped fill out the case against French morals, French judgment, and French taste that had been building in Twain's mind for more than thirty years.[108]

IS HE DEAD? AND POPULAR TRADITIONS OF VAUDEVILLE AND MELODRAMA

Late nineteenth-century America was obsessed with dialect in many popular arts (a phenomenon Gavin Jones examines in his illuminating book, *Strange Talk: The Politics of Dialect Literature in Gilded Age America*). The foremost of these was vaudeville, the nation's most popular form of entertainment from the 1870s through the 1920s, a place where characters who spoke like Dutchy and O'Shaughnessy and Li-Hung-Chang in *Is He Dead?* were ubiquitous. Like Twain's Dutchy, "Dutch" characters in vaudeville shows said "vot," "vell," "vas," "dot" and "goot" for "what," "well," "was," "that" and "good"; they substituted "sh" for "s" sounds (as in "shteal" for "steal") and "p" for "b" sounds ("py chorge!"); they spoke in German- and Dutch-inflected cadences; and, when they got excited, they tended to emote in German ("Gott im Himmel!").[109] Twain may have encountered some of this stage dialect when he attended a performance at the Garrick in 1893, a New York theatre that featured shows relying heavily on dialect humor at the time.[110] Stock "Dutch" characters in vaudeville, however, resembled Twain's Dutchy only in their German origins and stereotyped speech. Vaudeville's "Dutch" characters tended to be ignorant clowns, while Twain's Dutchy is a smart, resourceful, and endearing figure.

The vaudeville stage, as well as the Chautauqua circuit, also abounded with characters who spoke in the Irish dialect spoken by Twain's Phelim O'Shaughnessy.[111] Chinese characters were also frequently portrayed on the vaudeville stage, identified by makeup and dress, but just as importantly by dialect resembling that spoken by Twain's Li-Hung-Chang. When Twain's Chang says "You go helly," "Me makee alle buy," "Mellican-man," and "I no leave Flançois," he sounds a lot like a Chinese character named Two-Hi in an 1895 vaudeville script called *The Geezer*, who says "she kick like hellee," "Me no li-kee him," and "Mellican woman." Twain's Chang says, "Flançois welly good fliend to Li-Hung-Chang," while a character in *The Geezer* addressing a young Chinese woman says, "I likee you too welly much."[112]

Despite surface similarities, however, between some of the dialect in *Is He Dead?* and that of vaudeville performances, the dialect serves a different purpose in Twain's play. While dialect and linguistic play in vaudeville, according to Jones, served often "to demean through laughter the otherness of foreign speech," the presence of "Dutch," "Chinese," and "Irish" stage dialect in *Is He Dead?* serves, rather, to emphasize the international nature of the enterprise in which these multiethnic artists and art students are engaged.[113] As Chicago remarks at one point, "great art, supreme art, has no nationality."

Interestingly, Twain may have taken the name "Li-Hung-Chang" from vaudeville—although he could just as easily have taken it from the headlines of the day's newspapers—for Li Hung-chang was *both* a famous Chinese official of whom Twain was aware *and* a common figure on the vaudeville stage, the latter reflecting the real Li Hung-chang's international visibility.[114] As one of the most famous Chinese figures in the West during the 1890s, Li Hung-chang was the inspiration for characters on the vaudeville stage who were supposed to be Chinese officials. He appears in Joseph Herbert's *The Geezer*, for example, as a powerful Chinese viceroy.[115] Li Hung-chang also appears as the central figure in an 1897 one-act burlesque comedy by W. C. Robey called *Li Hung Chang's Reception*.[116]

Vaudeville may have left its mark on *Is He Dead?* in other ways, as well. The opening curtain in *Is He Dead?* reveals the Chimney Sweep alone on the stage. While chimney sweeps are relatively rare in the rest of Twain's oeuvre, soot-covered chimney sweeps featured in a gag that was popular on the vaudeville stage.[117] Twain's Chimney Sweep leaves his "calling card" in soot on a white sheet that had been draped over a sofa, while the vaudeville Chimney Sweep leaves a cloud of soot on a flour-covered miller's white suit—but both scenarios use chimney sweeps to mine the sight-gag potential of soot on white cloth.[118]

Is He Dead? also captures the spirit of vaudeville on those three occasions when Chicago and his fellow artists and art students erupt into spontaneous celebratory dances. In response to having received large sums for the paintings from the San Francisco Nabob and the Englishman, a stage direction instructs Chicago and the other artists to "embrace—dance—pupils and all." In response to the news that "the King himself is going to the funeral!" Chicago "marches, playing trombone," while "the other three dance to each other an

A (In first page of)
Act I

Curtain exposes chimney sweep
sitting on a footstool, his head
bowed on his knees, asleep. He
gradually comes awake, yawns,
stretches, looks around. Begins
munching an apple. "No use
waiting any longer. - - - I was
~~ahead of time, now~~
behind time; now he'll say I didn't
come." (Gets up & stretches.) - .
"Leave my card. ~~come again.~~
It'll show I done his errand." (Searches
his seat-bag for card. Disappointed.)
"Not a visiting-card left." (Takes up
a paint-brush — is going to paint
his name on the canvas that covers
the Angelus.) "Leave my name.
- - - A-N - - - no, A-double-N - - -
no — don't know how to spell it."
(Throws down brush. Sees the white

sheet that covers the sofa. Nods
approval. Stretches himself out
on it. Rises & holds it up, exposing
his printed form, done in soot.
Hangs the sheet on the tall easel
of the Angelus.   Exit, R.

(Enter Dutchy.) — L.
Dutchy. (Examining sheet)
If dot sweep ton't come, it means
he can't find him — — and dot
would pe bad — mighty pad.
(Anxiously) I vish he vould come!
I vish he — (sees the sheet. Joyously)
Goot! he's peen here — — and it's
all right. (Admiring the soot-
print.) Ah. Dot is sphlennid —
sphlennid, for a fellow dot hain't
had no draining in Art. (Throws
the sheet clean-side up, & covers the
ragged sofa with it.)
(Enter the Leroux family & Chicago.
Melancholy hand. shaking with Dutchy.)

Manuscript pages A and B, in Mark Twain's own hand, are part of his revisions to the secretarial manuscript of *Is He Dead?* In his annotation at the end of the first paragraph in Act 1, Twain left these instructions for a future director or producer: "(Here insert pages A & B, or leave them out, as you choose. S L C)." Courtesy Mark Twain Papers, The Bancroft Library.

Irish jig." And to help cheer Millet's spirits after he has realized that he is destined to remain forever a "successful imitator of my own works," Chicago says, "Let's dance it off," and the stage direction tell us that "they all dance the can-can." These moments of jubilant élan set to music remind us of the vaudeville stage at its silly, exuberant best.

Is He Dead? also embraces traditions of melodrama popular on the nineteenth-century American, French, and English stage. André's greed and villainy, the victimization of the innocent Leroux family and Millet, the attempted suicide involving carbon monoxide fumes from a lit charcoal heater, and Millet's triumph in the end, would have struck turn-of-the-century audiences as redolent of popular melodrama. One of the leading playwrights who fed nineteenth-century America's appetite for melodrama was the versatile Dion Boucicault (whom Twain and Warner had initially tried to enlist to dramatize *The Gilded Age* and whose legal battles over copyright issues Twain followed with interest).[119] Boucicault, a dramatist of Irish and French ancestry, was a master at adapting European melodramas for American tastes. The idea that suicide is preferable to slow death by starvation features prominently in one of Boucicault's best-known melodramas, *The Poor of New York,* adapted from *Les Pauvres de Paris* by Édouard Brisebarre and Eugène Nus. One critic notes that the French original was inspired by "a popular narrative painting of the time, Octave Tassaert's 'An Unfortunate Family, or the Suicide,' showing a destitute mother and daughter in a miserable garret awaiting death from the carbon monoxide fumes of a charcoal heater." But while the original French play climaxed with the attempted suicide, Boucicault downplayed it in the American version, making it simply the prelude to the play's real climax—a change that reflected the fact that American melodramatic heroes and heroines "fight back, get to work, start a new life. . . ." In Boucicault's play, the starving innocent's attempted suicide through inhalation of fumes from a charcoal brazier is thwarted by a friend who bursts into the room and breaks the window, while in Twain's play, Chicago thwarts a similar suicide attempt by throwing open the doors. Boucicault's play features a villainous love-struck banker who tries to squeeze his victims dry on technicalities, much as André tries to find legal loopholes that allow him to ruin Millet, the Leroux family, and the other artists. Boucicault's play, under the numerous titles he gave the various versions he produced in England and the United States, was the most widely performed of all of this popular dramatist's works throughout the nineteenth century.[120]

The Manichean "clash of virtue and villainy," as Peter Brooks characterizes the engine that drives melodrama, activates the plot of *Is He Dead?* André is the embodiment of evil, while Marie, the Leroux family, and Millet and his fellow artists are good, kind, persecuted innocents. On the melodramatic stage, as Daniel Gerould has noted, "the destitute can become wealthy; the persecuted and beleaguered can start life fresh and become someone new." That transformation, central to the action of *Is He Dead?* is fleshed out through Twain's detailed specifications about costumes and stage sets as well as through plot. The play's happy ending invites the kind of audience response that the authors of nineteenth-century melodramas typically sought: "We rejoice at [the hero's] luck, share vicariously in his triumphs, and leave the theatre ready to tackle the world single-handed and win."[121] Twain wrote *Is He Dead?* at precisely the moment he managed to extricate himself from the burdens of heavy debt; it is certainly possible that some of the pleasure he took in writing the play came from his identification with his characters' escape from penury and debt as well.

Although *Is He Dead?* draws on conventions of melodrama, it also turns them inside out. Take the scenario in which a usurer intends to foreclose on the family of a young woman who rejects his marriage proposal. The set-up may be familiar, but where Twain goes with it is fresh: by having the rival suitor "die," and then, in a transvestite reincarnation, become an alternative object of the villain's affections, Twain turns a cliché into a launching pad for his own distinctive brand of over-the-top comedy.

Twain combined two of the nineteenth century's most popular theatrical traditions, vaudeville and melodrama, in his efforts to craft "a play that would play"—one that might potentially appeal to a large popular audience.

IS HE DEAD? AND TRADITIONS OF MALE CROSS-DRESSING IN THE THEATRE

Men commonly played women in nineteenth-century popular entertainment in both the United States and England, despite the fact that women had been appearing as themselves on stage since around 1660. Female impersonators were stock figures in pantomimes, minstrel shows, burlesque, vaudeville, and popular comedies, as well as in amateur theatricals.[122] Indeed, male cross-dressing was central to the play that was probably the biggest worldwide hit of the 1890s, Brandon Thomas's *Charley's Aunt*. Although we do not have a complete inventory of the plays and popular entertainment Twain attended, there is reason to assume that a good deal of this repertoire was familiar to him. In certain respects, *Is He Dead?* conforms to contemporary traditions of men playing women on the stage, while in other ways, it goes beyond them.

One critic dates female impersonation in America to the late 1840s, when minstrels donned women's clothing to portray credible romantic characters— the "prima donna" or "wench" role. George Christy, for example, of the Christy Minstrels (whose shows Twain recalled with pleasure) performed the flirtatious song "Lucy Long" in drag, elegantly attired as a woman.[123] The "prima donna" was refined and delicate. "With fluttering eyelashes and hearts," one critic writes, "they flirted behind their fans, occasionally allowing their beaus to steal kisses."[124] The New York *Clipper*, a popular theatrical journal of the day, observed that Francis Leon, one of the most famous actors who performed this stock role, "does it with such dignity, modesty, and refinement, that it is truly art." Leon prided himself on the fact "that he did absolutely nothing offensive or vulgar."[125] Twain may have had a figure like Leon in the back of his mind when he wrote that he intended "the Widow Tillou to be a lady—a lady subject to accidents and mistakes and awkwardnesses in her unaccustomed costume, but still at heart a lady."

Leon was far from the only successful female impersonator on the American stage. Neil Burgess popularized another stock role, the comic "dame," that may have left its mark on the Widow Tillou character. Boston-born Burgess assumed his first female role when called on to replace an actress who had suddenly fallen ill in a Providence, Rhode Island, production of a farce; his performance was so popular that he began playing women in vaudeville shows.[126] An 1876 ad for Tony Pastor's theatre in the New York *Herald* proclaimed Burgess to be the "unapproachable delineator of eccentric females."[127] He soon developed full-length plays to showcase his female impersonations. One of his most famous roles was the Widow Bedott, a warmhearted, sharp-tongued older woman in an 1879 play of that name, *The Widow Bedott Papers*. Also popular were his performances in similar roles in *Josiah Allen's Wife* (or, as it was later called, *Vim*) and *The County Fair*. Burgess wrote Twain the day he performed in *Vim* in Hartford on October 28, 1884, enclosing free tickets for the show.[128] Twain and his wife were unable to accept, but the exchange of letters shows that Twain would have been aware of Burgess and his act, as does Twain's brief mention of Burgess's new play, *The County Fair*, in a notebook from the late 1880s.[129] Burgess toured the country with these plays in the 1880s and 1890s, performing to capacity audiences and critical acclaim. Burgess's female characters were less refined and genteel than Leon's, and more comic. But far from presenting low-comedy clowns, Burgess, like Leon, was praised for presenting "personations" that were "very artistic and quite free from vulgarity."[130] Laurence Senelick notes that "although the long-standing tradition of the dame, an elderly woman played by a man, survived in burlesque comedy, Burgess assimilated it to the legitimate stage through his realism and avoidance of the suggestive."[131]

Unlike the "prima donna" character who aspires to a complete, unbroken illusion of being female, the "dame's" underlying maleness is never completely hidden from the audience's awareness. Twain may have had this tradition in mind when, during her first scene in the play, the Widow—"young, handsome, cheaply but prettily dressed"—comes "mincing out of the bedroom, smoking a corncob or briarwood pipe" (later in the play Marie complains about the Widow's smoking). Burgess was so successful in these roles that his performances inspired numerous other male actors to appear in "widder shows" or present "widder" characters throughout this period.[132] Burgess's *County Fair* caused a sensation in the late 1880s not because of his portrayal of the "dame" character Abigail Prue, but because it featured a memorable special effect: an onstage horse race featuring real horses running on a special treadmill Burgess patented himself. Fourteen years after its debut, the show celebrated 5,000 performances. Senelick notes that the play "was seen in every American town that boasted a playing space, and made Burgess one of America's richest actors."[133] Twain loved theatrical special effects—indeed, his play *Colonel Sellers as a Scientist* was built out of them—and would probably have paid attention to press notices of Burgess's wildly successful adventures for this reason alone, even if he never contemplated putting a Widow character of his own on stage. The Players, a club for actors and others who cared about the theatre, was founded by Edwin Booth, Augustin Daly, Laurence Hutton, Twain, and others in 1888—the same year that *County Fair* took the world of popular theatre by storm. Indeed, Burgess himself became one of the club's prominent members some time after its founding and would have had occasion to meet Twain during one of Twain's frequent stays there.[134] Twain was undoubtedly aware of Burgess's famous comic female impersonations.

And it would have been impossible for Twain to have been unaware of Brandon Thomas's play *Charley's Aunt*. Charles Frohman brought it to New York in October 1893, after a London run of 1,469 consecutive performances, and it quickly became the talk of the town. By the time it opened in New York, the playwright's son recalled, "*Charley's Aunt* had become a craze. All kinds of souvenirs were made in its honor—there were *Charley's Aunt* paper-knives, ink bottles, nibs, dolls, pen wipers." It would become the most popular British play of the nineteenth century and, in one critic's view, "one of the most successful plays of all time."[135] Within months of its New York opening, there were nine touring companies performing the play in the United States, seven in Germany, and four in Britain. Soon the play was touring successfully in New Zealand, Australia, South Africa, and Canada. A Greek production opened in Athens in 1894, and productions were mounted shortly thereafter in Austria and Germany. Typical of reviewers' comments was that of the *New York Times* critic who called Thomas's farce "a great and real success, immensely and intensely funny, in thorough good taste from beginning to end, and in certain features refreshingly original. . . ."[136] *Charley's Aunt* was precisely the kind of theatrical success to which Twain himself aspired.

When *Charley's Aunt* opened in New York, Twain was living at the Players club, attending the theatre regularly and spending a substantial portion of his time dining, drinking, and playing billiards with actors and producers.[137] One actor who "loved and often frequented" the Players club that season (and who may well have encountered Twain there) was Etienne Girardot, the star of *Charley's Aunt*, whose cross-dressing impersonation of a widow dissolved the audience in laughter night after night at the Standard Theatre.[138] It is also highly likely that Twain met Brandon Thomas, the play's author, at some point in the 1890s, since they shared both membership in a club (the Savage Club, the favorite London club of both Thomas and Twain) and a good friend (the actor Sir Henry Irving).[139] In any event, Twain could not have missed the barrage of glowing reviews that filled the New York papers when *Charley's Aunt* opened or the notices attesting to the play's worldwide success throughout the 1890s.

The plot of *Charley's Aunt* is this: two Oxford undergraduates have invited young ladies to a lunch that is to be chaperoned by Charley's Aunt in an era when a chaperone is de rigueur for such gatherings. They panic when the Aunt is delayed, since they are loathe to cancel what will be their last chance to see the girls before summer vacation. Lord Fancourt Babberly, a classmate who has just gotten the woman's costume he is to wear in a college theatrical, turns up at just the right (or wrong) moment and is forced by his friends to impersonate Charley's Aunt for the afternoon. Delightful havoc ensues.

Charley's Aunt and *Is He Dead?* are set in different times (Oxford, England, in the 1890s versus Barbizon, France, in the 1840s) and have very different sets of characters. *Is He Dead?* embraces more social satire and explores more serious issues than *Charley's Aunt*. Yet for all these differences, some common elements remain. Both plays involve groups of young men who find themselves in a crisis that can be resolved only by one of their group donning women's clothes and impersonating a widow. The cross-dressing males have trouble in both cases remembering how women are expected to carry themselves, speak, and act. They both shock people around them by their habit of smoking. Both are pursued by unwanted suitors. And both are befuddled about how to respond to questions about their children. In *Charley's Aunt*, when Dona Lucia asks the cross-dressing Lord Fancourt Babberly, a.k.a. Babbs, whether she has any children, Babbs answers, "Only a few—none to speak of." In *Is He Dead?* when Madame Bathilde asks Millet, a.k.a. the Widow, whether she has any children, the Widow answers, "Slathers," leaving her visitors dazed.[140]

Laurence Senelick observes that *Charley's Aunt* was

> removed from *fin-de-siècle* decadence, the Woman Question, divorce or any social problems current in drama. . . . In a period when French farce had to be disinfected of its sexual content before it could be admitted onto English-speaking stages, *Charley's Aunt*, which owes nothing to a Gallic original, is "good clean fun," pivoting sentimentally on engagements and marriages. . . . Much of the comedy arises from Lord Fancourt Babberly's being a transvestite *malgré lui*; his initial discomfort in the role of a spinster aunt [turns] to a mischievous glee in fooling his obnoxious suitors. . . .[141]

One could say much the same about *Is He Dead?*—a farce set in France that required no "disinfecting," a play largely removed from current social problems, where much of the comedy stems from watching Millet move from "initial discomfort" to "a mischievous glee in fooling his obnoxious suitor." In a similar vein, theatre historian Jeffrey Huberman has commented that *"Charley's Aunt* is one of the few late Victorian farces that is not concerned with the domestic imbroglios of marriage."[142] The play's huge success showed that preoccupation with "the domestic imbroglios of marriage" was not a prerequisite for a successful farce and may well have encouraged Twain to try his hand at this genre in the late 1890s.

Perhaps the greatest similarity between *Charley's Aunt* and *Is He Dead?* lies in the character, demeanor, and carriage of the cross-dressed protagonist. Brandon Thomas said approvingly of W. S. Penley, the actor who inaugurated the title role in his play, that "he is unerring refinement."[143] Drama critics concurred. "In all such impersonations the besetting danger is vulgarity of treatment or suggestion," one critic wrote; "this Mr. Penley contrives to avoid."[144] Twain clearly sought a similar portrayal of his own cross-dressed protagonist when he specified that the Widow Tillou should be, despite her accidents and awkwardnesses, "a lady." The phenomenal success of *Charley's Aunt* in England, America, and around the world in the 1890s may well have helped inspire Twain to write his own clean, farcical comedy in which a cross-dressing character played a central role.

MARK TWAIN'S UNSUCCESSFUL EFFORTS TO GET *IS HE DEAD?* PRODUCED

Soon after Twain finished *Is He Dead?* he sent it off to Bram Stoker, who had agreed some time earlier to be his dramatic agent in Britain. Stoker had published his own very successful novel, *Dracula*, the year before and had been good friends with Twain for at least fifteen years. The two were brought together by their mutual interest in the theatre and by their devotion to the great British actor Sir Henry Irving. Stoker had worked for the actor since 1877, when Irving first hired him as his personal agent-manager and manager of the Lyceum, the theatre Irving had leased in London for his new company. Stoker (and Irving) had invested in the Paige typesetting machine on Twain's recommendation (much to Twain's later chagrin), but the friendship survived the financial loss when the machine failed. Twain and Stoker had spent time together in New York, at the Players club, and in London, where Twain had rented a house in Tedworth Square near the Stokers' St. Leonard's Terrace home as he finished writing *Following the Equator* in 1897. During the dark months following the death of Twain's daughter Susy, when Twain had kept generally to himself, Stoker was one of the friends who fed him dinner and helped keep his spirits up.[145]

In early 1898, when Twain approached Stoker about placing his plays, Stoker was at the peak of his career, having built the Lyceum into one of the most thriving and respected theatres in London and having just published a successful popular novel of his own. His primary responsibility was acting as Irving's agent and managing the Lyceum; writing and promoting his own books had first claim on whatever energy he had left. Nonetheless, Stoker agreed to be the British agent for Twain's plays, for a 15 percent commission.[146] Twain was pleased. The two had great personal rapport, and he couldn't have picked an agent with better connections in the world of London theatre. It was with high hopes then that in February 1898, Twain sent *Is He Dead?* to Stoker.[147]

His timing could not have been worse. On February 18, Stoker suffered a crushing and unexpected blow that signaled the end of life as he had known it in the theatre. He was woken up at 5:10 A.M. that morning by a cab driver bringing an urgent message from the Bow Street police station. A fire had broken out in the Lyceum's rented storage area on Bear Lane in Southwark. The cab raced Stoker to the scene, getting him there in time to watch the Lyceum's accumulated scenery of two decades—260 scenes for forty-four plays, more than 2,000 pieces of scenery, along with the corresponding costumes and props—go up in flames. Everything was destroyed. To make matters worse, as an economy measure, Irving had reduced the theatre's insurance coverage just months before, leaving £50,000 worth of scenery and props insured for a small fraction of their worth.[148] But, Stoker wrote, the financial disaster "was the least part of the loss. Nothing could repay the time and labour and artistic experience" that the sets and props represented: "All the scene painters in England working for a whole year could not have restored the scenery alone." For Irving, as Stoker recalled, it meant "the deprivation of all that he had built up."[149] As one of Stoker's biographers notes, Irving "took it very hard. Now, more than ever, he retreated into his shell, leaving [Stoker] to deal with everyday business. . . ." In the memoir he wrote about Irving, Stoker called the fire of February 1898 "permanently disastrous."[150]

By early March, Twain had Stoker's initial response to *Is He Dead?*—"On a first reading he doesn't much believe in my play, but says he is going to examine it more closely."[151] He thought it might be good "for America, possibly—not for England."[152] Twain took Stoker's lack of encouragement at face value, apparently unaware of the devastating loss that might have made him cool, at the time, toward any future project on the stage. By mid-March Twain was complaining that he was "tired of Stoker; he promises with energy, but is too slow and uncertain and unsatisfactory."[153] If Stoker ever gave Twain's play the closer reading he promised, we have no record of it. His own problems, which got even more severe during the next few years, probably claimed his full attention.[154]

Twain then asked his friends Henry Huttleston Rogers and C. C. Rice, M.D. (who had introduced him to Rogers some years earlier), to help him try to place the play in the United States. Stoker's lack of interest shook Twain's confidence in his project. He began referring to *Is He Dead?* as "my so-called play" and decided he'd probably never place it in its current form. Twain wrote Rogers that if "my so-called play . . . were put into the hands of a professional playwright it might perhaps be made a playing piece. An American one, I mean." He suggested that Rogers contact Charles Frohman, one of the most powerful theatre impresarios in the country, about finding such a person. Some months later, when Frohman himself expressed interest in seeing the play, Twain asked Rogers to send it to him.[155]

Rice tried to interest Alf Hayman, who was manager of Charles Frohman's traveling companies. It was Charles Frohman who had brought *Charley's Aunt* to New York and who had orchestrated its hugely successful tour. Just the man to do something with *Is He Dead?* Rice must have thought—and also with the other Viennese plays Twain was translating. But Frohman's man didn't bite. On February 27, 1899, he informed Rice of his decision about the three plays Rice had sent him. "I am at last in a position to write you intelligently concerning Mark Twain's three plays—'Is He Dead,' 'Bartel Turaser' and 'In Purgatory,'" Hayman wrote. He judged that *Bartel Turaser,* Twain's translation of a play then popular on the Viennese stage, was "what is known as a problem play, suitable only to an actor like Richard Mansfield." Hayman added that he had submitted the play "to quite a number of managers who could not see anything in it. Mansfield had it for nearly two months and returned it without comment." Hayman concluded that it would not be "possible to place it here." Hayman sent *In Purgatory,* another translation, to Charles Frohman himself in London (Frohman found it "all jabber & no play").[156]

Hayman showed it to other managers as well and wrote Rice that he had left it with "Wm. Harris, of Rich & Harris, big play producers who has promised to let me have a decision regarding it in a few days." But Hayman thought better of *Is He Dead?*—the one original play in the batch:

> This is unquestionably the best work of the three, according to all opinions. The enclosed letter from Klaw and Erlanger will be interesting.
>
> You will doubtless wonder why I have taken so long a time to let you hear from me regarding these plays, but it's an awfully hard matter to get a manager or actor of any standing to read a play and when they do it's a matter of a month or two before the manuscript is returned. Unless you desire to return the plays to Mr. Twain I suggest you let me keep them a little while longer. Perhaps something may turn up. . . .[157]

As it turned out, nothing did turn up—although the managers at Klaw and Erlanger thought the play definitely had possibilities. They wrote Hayman: "it strikes us that if that play were revised by some clever and practical dramatist, particularly in the last act, that there is a favorable opportunity for it. The idea is certainly unique and the treatment of some of the scenes very humorous."[158] Perhaps they hoped a "clever and practical dramatist" would figure out a way to trim the unusually large cast, particularly given the scene in the last act that directed "the entire dramatis personae" to "come filing solemnly in, announced, name by name, by a Splendid Flunkey." The requirement that the entire large cast assemble on stage at the same time would have limited the prospects of doubling too many roles, thereby adding a lot to the overall cost of the production. As late as April 1899, Twain continued to express his hopes that the play would be produced: "I wish Rice would redramatise 'Is He Dead.' It would keep him out of mischief, and shorten his gambling-hours, and postpone the gallows; and *I* know, quite well, that that play will never play until it is reconstructed."[159] Twain does not seem to have persisted in trying to get the play produced, perhaps because he sensed that the current climate in the theatre was not favorable.

Charley's Aunt ended its four-year run in London in December 1896, but performances continued around the world. In the century that followed, it would become the "most revived farce in modern times."[160] Five years after he launched *Charley's Aunt* in America with great success, Charles Frohman was given the chance to produce *Is He Dead?* a play that resembled it in several ways. Why did he turn it down? And (leaving aside for a moment the personal disaster that may have clouded his judgment), why did Bram Stoker think he couldn't place the play on the British stage?

One explanation may be that by 1898, the theatre scene had changed dramatically. Twain came along at the tail end of a bubble that had burst: farcical comedy had run its course during the 1890s on both sides of the Atlantic. Critic Jeffrey Huberman has called *Charley's Aunt* "the last great Victorian farce."[161] Right after its triumph, the form went into decline. By 1898 farce was simply no longer popular. Huberman tells us that

> In the last seven years of the nineteenth century, full-length British farce declined in popularity almost as quickly as it had appeared in 1875. Without the perspective of history, theatrical producers saw the success of *Charley's Aunt* as the dawn of yet another new age of farce popularity. They assumed that *Charley's Aunt* was the formula. In the hands of hack writers looking to turn a quick profit, farce became imitative rather than derivative. At first the public accepted one or two of the better *Charley's Aunt* imitations, but the formula soon became overly familiar and, on the whole, theatre-goers began to lose interest—despite the initial rush to produce more farces. . . . The reality of the situation was that public enthusiasm for the full-length farce began to decline rapidly in the last five years of the century. . . .[162]

Twain's farcical comedy was original. Even the theatrical syndicate that sent a rejection letter to Frohman's agent had to admit that the idea of the play was "certainly unique."[163] But the moment had passed. The supply of farces had outstripped the demand, and the saturated market stopped buying. In Britain, naturalistic foreign plays, Shavian comedy, and "problem plays" were in ascendance; farce was out.[164] The situation was much the same in New York, where, as Twain heard in June 1898, "war-plays" were currently all the rage.[165] Perhaps the Spanish-American War had pushed the theatre in a more patriotic direction. In any case, plays with titles like *The Man-o'-War's Man* and *Battles of Our Nation* filled the theatres now. "Everything literary here is filled with the din of arms," Howells wrote Twain that August.[166] Twain wasn't the only dramatist not getting produced: by 1898, authors of many of the successful farces of the early 1890s could not get their new plays on stage either.[167] Twain's response was to give up on the theatre, largely abandoning the dream he had had since the 1870s of writing another hit play.[168]

Another possible explanation for Twain's difficulty in getting *Is He Dead?* produced may stem from a key way in which Twain's play differed from *Charley's Aunt*. Thomas's Lord Fancourt Babberly was a fictitious Oxford undergraduate, but Twain's Millet was the "real" Jean-François Millet, painter of the celebrated paintings *The Angelus*, *The Gleaners*, and *The Sower* and a venerated cultural icon. It was one thing for a male Oxford undergraduate in *Charley's Aunt* to don women's clothes, but it was quite another thing to dress Jean-François Millet, one of France's greatest painters, in drag for two acts. Although Millet/The Widow is presented respectfully, traditionalists might have felt that seeing the great painter in drag was disrespectful, no matter how refined the lady was. Neither in Britain nor the United States had any of the Widow's cross-dressed predecessors in either legitimate theatres or more popular venues portrayed real historical figures. They were always invented characters. Twain's decision to cast such a towering figure in the arts in drag and show him engaging in demonstrations of affection—however feigned—with a repulsive male art dealer, may well have been too audacious and transgressive for 1898.

WHY A PLAY THAT WOULDN'T PLAY IN THE 1890s MIGHT PLAY TODAY

Although *Is He Dead?* may have been out of step with the theatre trends of the late 1890s, today we are free to see the play for the surprising work that it is.

In terms of the arc of Twain's life and career, *Is He Dead?* is particularly interesting because its high-spirited energy runs counter to the dominant image of Twain's writing during this period—a time when he produced, according to the conventional wisdom, mainly works of dark, brooding pessimism and grim determinism. Bernard DeVoto described the work of Twain's later years as most often focused on the themes of "man's complete helplessness in the grip of the inexorable forces of the universe, and man's essential cowardice, pettiness and evil," while Forrest Robinson writes that during this period Twain's "Olympian relish for the bounty of creation had given way almost completely to determinism, nihilism, despair."[169] But Chicago, Dutchy, and Millet are not helpless, cowardly, petty, or evil; on the contrary, they are resourceful, boldly inventive, generous, and good. And rather than reflecting a world ruled by determinism, nihilism, and despair, *Is He Dead?* evokes a world in which imagination, chutzpah, and collective action trump malevolence and abusive power. There is something inspiring about the fact that

Twain was able to emerge from his slough of mourning and gloom with the resilience to write a play as zany and exuberant as this one. That feat is all the more poignant since we know the blows that are still to come—the death of his wife, the death of his youngest daughter, Jean, his sharp disillusionment with his country, his declining health.

This neglected work also gives us new perspective on the engagement with debates about authenticity and artifice that resonate throughout Twain's writings. Questions of who and what one really "is" come into play in *Is He Dead?* when Millet realizes, as he is about to come back as a young artist who paints in the style of Millet, that he is destined to spend his life as an "imitator of myself." Might a Mark Twain who often felt constrained to present to the world familiar versions of himself that the public held dear have also felt like an imitator of himself at times? As Forrest Robinson reminds us, "Clemens felt like a fake" needing to "look no further than his famous nom de plume for a reminder. . . ."[170] During this period he signed one hotel guest register, "S. L. Clemens, Profession, Mark Twain."[171] The question of authenticity and artifice in people is not unrelated to the questions of originals and copies in art that the play raises frequently as the young artists' scam wreaks havoc on the real identities of Millet's original paintings. Who's the "real" Millet? Which is the "real" *Angelus?* Who's authentic, and who's the imposter or claimant?[172] And will the "real" Mark Twain/Samuel Clemens please stand up? *Is He Dead?* complicates, in interesting ways, a theme that runs through virtually everything Twain ever wrote—the riddle of identity.

Also striking is the play's contribution to the Twain oeuvre of a memorable and distinctive character, the Widow Tillou. Women were central to Twain's creative process during his most productive and successful periods as a writer, and aesthetic strategies associated with women were central to his work, but he is not generally known for having created very many genuinely interesting female characters.[173] Although one might counter that Twain pushes beyond stereotypes with Laura Hawkins in *The Gilded Age*, Aunt Rachel in "A True Story," Joan in *Joan of Arc*, Roxy in *Pudd'nhead Wilson*, Eve in *Eve's Diary*, and Hellfire Hotchkiss in the posthumously published "Hellfire Hotchkiss Sequence," these are the exceptions.[174] In the Widow Daisy Tillou, Twain has created a "female character" who is sensitive, strategic, smart, kind and outspoken; a libidinous heterosexual male impeccably attired as a proper Victorian matron; a man pretending to be a woman, who both chafes under the restrictions of the role and revels in the opportunities for intimacy with his sweetheart that it affords him; a good-hearted leader of a band of talented young men and a sympathetic female friend of a young woman in mourning; a ditzy nonsense-spewing eccentric old lady and a woman who rises to heights of eloquence usually reserved, on the Victorian stage, for men. What other woman in nineteenth-century theatre had a speech as searing as that with which the Widow Tillou excoriates André at the close of the second act? Even the most outspoken women on the Victorian stage did not get to call the villain a "contemptible, base-begotten damned scoundrel!" But what does it mean that during the rise of the "New Woman," at a time when Twain himself was supporting women's suffrage and trying to write a play about women in politics, one of the most interesting female characters Twain created is really a man? What are we supposed to make of Millet's gender-bending masquerade?

This latter question intersects with a number of debates in the academy today—about the significance of drag, the nature of gender, the complex meanings of cross-dressing. Scholars including Laurence Senelick, Judith Butler, and Marjorie Garber have argued that drag can help unmask the performative and constructed nature of gender roles.[175] "If essence of gender can be simulated through wigs, props, gestures, costumes, cross-dressing implies that it is not an essence at all, but an unstable construct," Senelick writes in *The Changing Room*.[176] While some critics accept the idea that cross-dressing can be a useful tool in the project of subverting gender stereotypes, others focus on drag's more potentially retrograde underside, suggesting that it always reinforces male power—or at least that it sends inherently mixed signals.[177] Twain's engaging, cross-dressing Millet/Daisy Tillou should provide new grist for this debate.

Is He Dead? may have been too "out there" for the Victorian 1890s, but it may be just right for the twenty-first century. The time may be right for audiences to enjoy Chicago's ingenuity and ebullience, the Widow's sly loopiness, the kindness and esprit de corps of the multiethnic crew of artists and art students, the send-up of the role of hype in the art world, the playful perspective on the "construction" of gender that we get from the Widow's gratifying revenge on André, the discussions of what makes "art" art, and the satisfyingly happy ending. Twain's well-crafted dialogue, subtle satire, appealing characters, and tightly structured plot pull it all together. The result is a champagne cocktail of a play—not too dry, not too sweet, with just the right amount of bubbles and buzz.

NOTES

FOREWORD

1. During the sixteen months following his daughter's death, Twain managed to finish a nonfiction travel book, *Following the Equator*, as well as some short fables, only one of which is known to have survived ("The Quarrel in the Strong-Box"). He began, but did not complete, imaginative fragments including the "Mysterious Stranger" manuscripts and "Hellfire Hotchkiss." As Albert Bigelow Paine, his first biographer, observed, "Clemens appeared to be at this time out of tune with fiction." Realizing that "various literary projects" he began during this period "were leading nowhere," Twain dropped them "one after another." Albert Bigelow Paine, *Mark Twain: A Biography*, 3 vols. (New York: Harper & Brothers, 1912), vol. 2, p. 1045.

2. Samuel Langhorne Clemens to William Dean Howells, 22 January 1898, in *Mark Twain–Howells Letters*, ed. Henry Nash Smith and William M. Gibson, 2 vols. (Cambridge: Harvard University Press, Belknap Press, 1960), vol. 2, p. 670.

3. Twain's bankruptcy was largely the result of his decision to invest huge sums in the Paige Compositor, an automatic typesetting machine. Twain was right when he assumed that automatic typesetting would be the technology of the future, but the machine on which he placed his bet did not become the industry standard. Although the Paige Compositor (not unlike the Betamax videotape) may even have been the superior technology, the Mergenthaler Linotype machine (the VHS of its day, to complete the analogy) was the one that newspapers ended up adopting. Twain lost all that he had invested. He embarked on a worldwide lecture tour to help pay his debts, gave up the family home in Hartford, Conn., and moved to Europe to save expenses.

4. Samuel Langhorne Clemens to Henry Huttleston Rogers, 10–11 November 1897, in *Mark Twain's Correspondence with Henry Huttleston Rogers, 1893–1909*, ed. Lewis Leary (Berkeley: University of California Press, 1969), p. 303 (emphasis in original); and postscript from Clemens in Olivia Langdon Clemens to Rogers, 17 November 1897, in Leary, *Correspondence with Rogers*, p. 305.

5. Clara Clemens, *My Father, Mark Twain* (New York: Harper & Brothers, 1931), p. 190; Clemens to Rogers, 8 October 1897 and 16 December 1897, in Leary, *Correspondence with Rogers*, pp. 302, 307–8; and Paine, *Biography*, vol. 2, pp. 1052, 1053. In his comment to Francis E. Bliss, his publisher, Twain added, "It would surprise (and gratify) me if I should be able to get another book ready for the press within the next three years." Albert Bigelow

Paine, *Mark Twain's Letters*, 2 vols. (New York: Harper & Brothers, 1917), vol. 2, p. 650. Twain's letter to his publisher was quoted in part in the *Critic* 28 (18 December 1897): 384 and also in the *Academy* 53 (1 January 1898): 12, citing the *Critic* as its source.

6. Notebook 42 (June 1897–March 1900), typescript p. 53, in the Mark Twain Papers (also available in *Microfilm Edition of Mark Twain's Literary Manuscripts Available in the Mark Twain Papers* [Berkeley: The Bancroft Library, 2002], vol. 33); Clemens to Rogers, 20 January 1898, in Leary, *Correspondence with Rogers*, p. 316 (emphasis in original). "By the end of January, 1898, Mark Twain had accumulated enough money to make the final payment to his creditors and stand clear of debt" (Paine, *Biography*, vol. 2, p. 1056). The royalties from *Following the Equator*, published in November 1897, also helped considerably. Within five months of its publication, Twain's travel book had sold 28,500 copies in the United States. Everett Emerson, *The Authentic Mark Twain: A Literary Biography* (Philadelphia: University of Pennsylvania Press, 1985), p. 209.

7. Clemens to Howells, 22 January 1898, Smith and Gibson, *Twain-Howells Letters*, vol. 2, p. 670; Clemens to Rogers, 5–6 February 1898, Leary, *Correspondence with Rogers*, p. 318. Twain told Rogers that "an Austrian professional dramatist came along and proposed to write an American comedy with me (woman in politics) on half-profit basis; and that comedy is about finished, now—it won't take many more days. Meantime I have translated a new and strong Austrian melancholy drama and secured the English and American rights on a half-profit basis. And between-times I have written a comedy by myself, entitled 'Is He Dead?'—and I put on the finishing touches to-day. . . ." Of *Is He Dead?* Twain added, "I think, myself, that for an ignorant first attempt it lacks a good deal of being bad. I am learning the trade pretty fast—I shall get the hang of it yet, I believe. I shall stick to the business right along until I either turn out something real good or find out I can't." Clemens to Rogers, 5 February 1898, Leary, *Correspondence with Rogers*, p. 318.

8. *Times* Weekly Edition (London), 4 February 1898, p. 77; cited in Smith and Gibson, *Twain-Howells Letters*, vol. 2, p. 671n4; Clemens to Rogers, 7 March 1898, Leary, *Correspondence with Rogers*, pp. 323, 325n1; Clemens to Rogers, 28 August 1898, Leary, *Correspondence with Rogers*, p. 358. After his comment expressing his hope that "someone should succeed in making a play out of 'Is He Dead?'" Twain added, "From what I gather from dramatists, he will have his hands something more than full—but let him struggle, let him struggle" (Clemens to Rogers, 17 November 1898, Leary, *Correspondence with Rogers*, p. 378).

9. For a full discussion of these factors, see Afterword, pp. 196–201.

10. Occasionally a scholar interested in Mark Twain and Vienna or Mark Twain and the theatre has glanced at the manuscript (a secretarial copy with additions and corrections in Twain's handwriting) in the archives of the Mark Twain Papers at The Bancroft Library at the University of California, Berkeley, but the play has never received more than a brief discussion. The play is mentioned or briefly discussed in Carl Dolmetsch, *"Our Famous Guest": Mark Twain in Vienna* (Athens: University of Georgia Press, 1992), pp. 119–21; Robert Goldman, "Mark Twain as Playwright," in *Mark Twain: A Sumptuous Variety*, ed. Robert Giddings (Totowa, N.J.: Vision and Barnes & Noble, 1985), pp. 121, 124; William R. Macnaughton, *Mark Twain's Last Years as a Writer* (Columbia: University of Missouri Press, 1979), pp. 77–79; Thomas Schirer, *Mark Twain and the Theatre* (Nuremburg: Hans Carl, 1984), pp. 95, 97, 100; and Everett Emerson, *The Authentic Mark Twain* (Philadelphia: Uni-

versity of Pennsylvania Press, 1985), p. 217. Twain never tried to get *Is He Dead?* published (although he tried for over a year to get it produced). If a letter he wrote to London-based journalist Frank Marshall White on 4 February 1898 from Vienna refers to this play, it would shed light on a possible reason why Twain did not publish it. However, it is more than likely that this letter refers to *Der Gegenkandidat, oder die Frauen Politiker*, a comedy on which Twain was collaborating with Viennese playwright Siegmund Schlesinger during this same period: "It wouldn't do to print the Comedy, because it would destroy the stage-right in England & could damage it in America. That would be rather sorrowful, after all the work I have put on it. . . ." Clemens to White, 4 February 1898, in Alderman Library, University of Virginia; published in *Microfilm Edition of Mark Twain's Previously Unpublished Letters* (Berkeley: The Bancroft Library, 2002), vol. 8.

11. Many of the short works Twain wrote or completed after January 1898 (including several that were published posthumously) are reprinted in *Mark Twain: Collected Tales, Sketches, Speeches, & Essays, 1891–1910*, ed. Louis J. Budd (New York: Library of America, 1992). Most of the full-length books Twain published during these years are included in the twenty-nine-volume Oxford Mark Twain, edited by Shelley Fisher Fishkin (New York: Oxford University Press, 1996). Other works from this final period in Twain's life may be found in *Europe and Elsewhere*, ed. Albert Bigelow Paine (New York: Harper & Brothers, 1923); *Mark Twain in Eruption: Hitherto Unpublished Pages about Men and Events*, ed. Bernard DeVoto (New York: Harper & Brothers, 1940); *Letters from the Earth*, ed. Bernard DeVoto (New York: Harper & Row, 1962); *Which Was the Dream? and Other Symbolic Writings of the Later Years*, ed. John S. Tuckey (Berkeley: University of California Press, 1967); *Mysterious Stranger Manuscripts*, ed. William M. Gibson (Berkeley: University of California Press, 1969); *Fables of Man*, ed. John S. Tuckey (Berkeley: University of California Press, 1972); *What Is Man? and Other Philosophical Writings*, ed. Paul Baender (Berkeley: University of California Press, 1973); *Mark Twain's Weapons of Satire: Anti-Imperialist Writings on the Philippine-American War*, ed. Jim Zwick (Syracuse: Syracuse University Press, 1992).

AFTERWORD

1. By far the fullest treatment of this subject is Thomas Schirer, *Mark Twain and the Theatre* (Nuremburg: Hans Carl, 1984), the only book on the topic. Other useful sources are *Mark Twain-Howells Letters*, ed. Henry Nash Smith and William M. Gibson, 2 vols. (Cambridge: Harvard University Press, Belknap Press, 1960); Albert Bigelow Paine, *Mark Twain: A Biography*, 3 vols. (New York: Harper and Brothers, 1912); *Mark Twain's Letters, Volume 6: 1874–1875*, ed. Michael B. Frank and Harriet Elinor Smith (Berkeley: University of California Press, 2002); *Mark Twain's Letters to His Publishers, 1867–1894*, ed. Hamlin Hill (Berkeley: University of California Press, 1967); Carl Dolmetsch, *"Our Famous Guest": Mark Twain in Vienna* (Athens: University of Georgia Press, 1992); *Mark Twain's Satires & Burlesques*, ed. Franklin R. Rogers (Berkeley: University of California Press, 1967); and Robert Goldman, "Mark Twain as a Playwright," in *Mark Twain: A Sumptuous Variety*, ed. Robert Giddings (Totowa, N.J.: Vision and Barnes & Noble, 1985), pp. 108–31. Cursory treatments of the subject may be found in Jerry W. Thomason, "Mark Twain as a Dramatist," in the *Mark Twain Encyclopedia*, ed. J. R. LeMaster and James D. Wilson (New York: Garland Publishing, 1993), pp. 228–30; Robert A. Wiggins, "Mark Twain and the Drama," *American*

Literature 25, no. 3 (November 1953): 279–86; and Rodman Gilder, "Mark Twain Detested the Theatre," *Theatre Arts* (January 1944), pp. 109–16. Unless otherwise noted, the scripts that were consulted for the plays mentioned in this essay are those in manuscript form in the Mark Twain Papers, The Bancroft Library, University of California, Berkeley.

2. Clemens to Pamela A. Moffett, 8 October 1853, *Mark Twain's Letters, Volume 1: 1853–1866,* ed. Edgar Marquess Branch, Michael B. Frank, Kenneth M. Sanderson, Harriet Elinor Smith, Lin Salamo, and Richard Bucci (Berkeley: University of California Press, 1988), p. 16. See Thomas Jefferson Snodgrass [Samuel L. Clemens], "Correspondence: St. Louis, October 18, 1856," *Keokuk Saturday Post,* 1 November 1856, p. 4, reprinted in *The Adventures of Thomas Jefferson Snodgrass,* ed. Charles Honce (Chicago: Pascal Covici, Publisher, 1928), pp. 3–16.

3. Schirer, *Twain and the Theatre,* pp. 12–13, 23–24.

4. Although Twain's letters are filled with references to plays and theatres he attended, a list of plays he was known to have seen has never been compiled. For more on Twain's dramatic criticism, see Sidney J. Krause, *Mark Twain as a Critic* (Baltimore: Johns Hopkins University Press, 1967). Twain participated frequently in amateur theatricals in Hartford as well as private theatricals with his family. (He once played Miles Hendon in a dramatization of *The Prince and the Pauper* presented for family and friends.) Actor Henry Irving told him he had missed his calling by not being an actor, and director/producer Augustin Daly tried without success to get him to act in a benefit performance in New York. See Paine, *Biography,* vol. 2, p. 571; Clara Clemens, "My Father," *Mentor* 12, no. 4 (May 1924): 21. When a minister refused to read a burial service for George Holland because he was an actor, Twain was outraged and launched into an impassioned defense of the acting profession. See *Galaxy Magazine,* February 1871, reprinted in Paine, *Biography,* vol. 3, Appendix, 1624–27. The Players, the brainchild of actor Edwin Booth, was founded in New York in 1888 and became a hub of social life for the men in the theatre and kindred arts. Booth purchased a brownstone at 16 Gramercy Park for the club, had it beautifully renovated by Stanford White, installed his collections of books and paintings, furnished it handsomely, and transferred the ownership of the house to the club. Twain stayed at the Players club frequently when in the city, and lived there from the fall of 1893 through the winter of 1894 (Paine, *Biography,* vol. 2, p. 867). As theatre impresario Daniel Frohman described it, "The idea behind 'The Players' Club' was not to found a Bohemian resort, but a place where actors would be able to meet artists of other professions, and laymen interested in the arts and the theatre." *Daniel Frohman Presents: An Autobiography* (New York: Claude Kendall & Willoughby Sharp, 1935), p. 82.

5. Schirer, *Twain and the Theatre,* p. 38; Frank and Smith, *Twain's Letters,* vol. 6, p. 129n2. Hill, *Twain's Letters to His Publishers,* p. 76. Twain's sense that there might be money in dramatizing his fiction may have been kindled by Augustin Daly's presentation, three months earlier, of a series of sketches and tableaux very loosely based on Twain's travel book *Roughing It,* published the previous year (Schirer, *Twain and the Theatre,* p. 38).

6. Twain seems to have put some time instead into writing a burlesque version of *Hamlet,* a project that occurred to him after attending a November 1873 performance of *Hamlet* featuring the actor Edwin Booth. See Rogers, *Twain's Satires & Burlesques,* pp. 49–86; and Paine, *Biography,* vol. 1, p. 495.

7. The San Francisco *Bulletin* announced on April 22 that the comic actor John T. Raymond would perform in "Mr. G. B. Densmore's dramatization of Mark Twain's latest satire, in four acts and a prologue, entitled 'The Gilded Age.'" San Francisco *Bulletin*, 22 April 1874, p. 4, quoted in Schirer, *Twain and the Theatre*, p. 41. See also Frank and Smith, *Twain's Letters*, vol. 6, pp. 126–27, 128–29, 128–29nn1–4; Clemens to Charles Dudley Warner, 5 May 1874, Frank and Smith, *Twain's Letters*, vol. 6, pp. 126–27 and also pp. 128–29; Schirer, *Twain and the Theatre*, pp. 38, 41; Paine, *Biography*, vol. 1, p. 518; Hill, *Twain's Letters to His Publishers*, p. 76. Twain paid Densmore $200 (with promises to send more if the play was successful). Twain did, in fact, later send Densmore more money as the play proved to be a great success. Densmore was satisfied with the arrangement.

8. Twain changed the name of the play in recognition of the fact that the title "The Gilded Age" rightly belonged to the collaborative venture with Warner, while Colonel Sellers was solely Twain's invention. Clemens to Howells, 20 September 1874, Frank and Smith, *Twain's Letters*, vol. 6, p. 233. A friend recalled the source of Twain's dissatisfaction with Raymond's performance: "The pathos of the part, and not its comic aspects, had most impressed him. He designed and wrote it for Edwin Booth. From the first and always he was disgusted by Raymond's portrayal. Except for its amazing popularity and money-making quality, he would have withdrawn it from the stage. . . ." (quoted in Frank and Smith, *Twain's Letters*, vol. 6, p. 241n2). A typical Colonel Sellers speech: "Sellers. (*With mystery*) . . . There's a little operation in hogs, that I'm considering. Buy up all the hogs in the country, at an easy figure, and then just shut down on the slaughter houses till they come to our terms. See; the price must tower, tower—why a hog would become jewelry. I've calculated all the chances, and there's six millions in it at the lowest figure. Talk about style, keeping carriages, and all that sort of thing.! Why you'd hear a man say—'there goes old Smith—rich?—well he keeps his hog.'" *Colonel Sellers . . . play as performed by Mr Raymond*, act 2, scene 1, p. 17, in the Mark Twain Papers; also available in *Microfilm Edition of Mark Twain's Literary Manuscripts Available in the Mark Twain Papers*, vol. 42. In the copy of the play sent to the Copyright Office on 20 July 1874, immediately upon completion of the text, this speech read as follows: "Hogs. Now the idea is to buy up all the hogs in the country, shut down on the slaughter houses untill the butchers come to our terms, 'There's millions in it.' Millions in it. Why Hogs! Hogs will become jewelry." *Colonel Sellers: A Drama in Five Acts*, p. 39, manuscript PS1322.C6, Library of Congress, 1874. Theatre impresario Daniel Frohman recalls in his memoirs that "The famous catch phrase 'There's millions in it!' came from the character of Colonel Sellers in Twain's play." Daniel Frohman, *Memories of a Manager* (London: William Heinemann, 1911), p. 49, cited in Schirer, *Twain and the Theatre*, p. 56.

9. George C. D. Odell, *Annals of the New York Stage*, vol. 9, p. 556, quoted in Schirer, *Twain and the Theatre*, p. 45. "The Park Theatre," *New York Tribune*, 18 September 1874, p. 4, quoted in Frank and Smith, *Twain's Letters*, vol. 6, p. 235n2. Additional reviews of *The Gilded Age* are reproduced in Frank and Smith, *Twain's Letters*, vol. 6, pp. 645–54. Brander Matthews, *Playwrights on Playmaking* (New York: Charles Scribner's Sons, 1923), pp. 169–71. Clemens to Charles J. Langdon, 19 March 1875, Frank and Smith, *Twain's Letters*, vol. 6, p. 420.

10. Paine, *Biography*, vol. 2, p. 587; Schirer, *Twain and the Theatre*, p. 62. For the text of the play, see *Ah Sin, A Dramatic Work by Mark Twain and Bret Harte*, ed. Frederick Anderson (San

Francisco: The Book Club of California, 1961). Twain's speech quoted in Joseph F. Daly, *The Life of Augustin Daly* (New York: Macmillan, 1917), pp. 235–36. C. T. Parsloe to Clemens, 5 August 1877, quoted in Schirer, *Twain and the Theatre*, p. 51. Clemens to Mollie Fairbanks, 6 August 1877, quoted in Everett Emerson, *The Authentic Mark Twain* (Philadelphia: University of Pennsylvania Press, 1985), p. 92.

11. Mark Twain and William Dean Howells, *Colonel Sellers as a Scientist*, in *The Complete Plays of W. D. Howells*, ed. Walter J. Meserve (New York: New York University Press, 1960), pp. 205–41. Goldman, "Mark Twain as a Playwright," p. 123. For Twain's notes on the saga of *Colonel Sellers as a Scientist*, see *Mark Twain's Notebooks & Journals, Volume 3 (1883–1891)*, ed. Frederick Anderson, Robert Pack Browning, Michael B. Frank, and Lin Salamo (Berkeley: The University of California Press, 1979), pp. 2, 13n21, 33n60, 35, 37–39, 195n46, 226, 237–239, 334, 337n106, and 342. Frohman, *Memories of a Manager*, p. 51. Frohman recalls that a theatre magazine of the day commented on the fiasco that "it may be taken for granted . . . that when [Mark Twain] gave Mr. Daniel Frohman $1,000 not to produce the new play . . . he came to the conclusion that, since he could not stand his own play, the public would not be likely to stand it." *The Theatre Magazine*, 31 May 1886, quoted in Daniel Frohman, *Encore* (New York: Lee Furman, 1937), pp. 107–8.

12. Schirer has observed that "Dramatics was far from a fleeting interest for Twain. He began at least eleven dramatizations by himself, was involved in ten different theatric collaborations and translated three plays from German into English. He also authorized other authors to dramatize seven of his novels." Schirer, *Twain and the Theatre*, p. 105. Twain often had to discourage unauthorized dramatizations of his work and sometimes found it necessary to take legal action against such productions. See Clemens to "Dear Sir," 8 September 1887 and Unmailed answer, 8 September 1887, in *Mark Twain's Letters*, ed. Albert Bigelow Paine, 2 vols. (New York: Harper & Brothers, 1917), vol. 2, pp. 476–79. There is neither time nor space here to give an overview of the successful dramatizations of Twain's work by others, a topic covered in Schirer's *Twain and the Theatre*, in all of the major biographies, and elsewhere. I have also limited my discussion of Twain's involvement in the theatre to the period before he wrote *Is He Dead?* and ignored such interesting activities during his later years as his support of the Actors' Fund and of the Children's Theatre sponsored by the Lower East Side's Educational Alliance.

13. These burlesques are included in Rogers, *Twain's Satires & Burlesques*: "Burlesque *Il Trovatore*," pp. 17–24; "Burlesque *Hamlet*," pp. 49–87; "Cap'n Simon Wheeler, The Amateur Detective. A Light Tragedy," pp. 216–89. Twain had written on the manuscript of *Meisterschaft* when he submitted it to *Century Magazine* in 1888, "There is some tolerably rancid German here and there in this piece. It is attributable to the proof-reader." But the comment was cut from the version that was published—perhaps by the proofreader. Paine, *Biography*, vol. 2, p. 849. After its initial publication in *Century Magazine*, Twain reprinted *Meisterschaft* in *Merry Tales* [1892], available in the Oxford Mark Twain edition, ed. Shelley Fisher Fishkin (New York: Oxford University Press, 1996), pp. 161–209. "Beau Brummel and Arabella" appears in Rogers, *Twain's Satires & Burlesques*, pp. 205–15. Twain's Notebook 28 (Browning, Frank, and Salamo, *Twain's Notebooks & Journals*, vol. 3, pp. 405–18) is filled with notes about a play to be based on Alphonse Daudet's melodramatic story about "an

ailing octogenarian veteran of Napoleon I's forces." Twain's notebook suggests that he completed this dramatization, but no manuscript is known to survive (Browning, Frank, and Salamo, *Twain's Notebooks & Journals*, vol. 3, p. 403). *The Death Wafer* was performed informally at New York's Carnegie Lyceum (Paine, *Biography*, vol. 3, p. 1194; Paine refers to it by the name of the story on which it was based, *The Death Disk*). The manuscript is in the Mark Twain Papers and is also available in *Microfilm Edition of Mark Twain's Literary Manuscripts Available in the Mark Twain Papers*, vol. 28. These other ideas are jotted down in Notebook 27 (renumbered in Mark Twain Papers as Notebook 33), typescript p. 38, quoted in Smith and Gibson, *Twain-Howells Letters*, vol. 2, p. 654n4. For the fate of Twain's collaborations with Howells, see Schirer, *Twain and the Theatre*, p. 72. Howells did, however, complete a number of plays on his own. "[H]e translated or adapted or wrote, in the end, thirty-six dramas, including a musical comedy." Smith and Gibson, *Twain-Howells Letters*, vol. 2, p. 463n2. Schirer believes that Twain may have first conceived of some of his best-known books—*Innocents Abroad, Tom Sawyer*—as plays. Schirer, *Twain and the Theatre*, p. 30.

14. Two indispensable studies of Twain's experiences with the theatre in Vienna are Dolmetsch, *Our Famous Guest*, chap. 6, pp. 109–31, and Schirer, *Twain and the Theatre*, chap. 11, pp. 94–101.

15. Stefan Zweig, *The World of Yesterday* (1943; reprint, Lincoln: University of Nebraska Press, 1964), p. 18, quoted in Dolmetsch, *Our Famous Guest*, p. 111.

16. *Neue Freie Presse*, 20 October 1897, p. 1, quoted in Dolmetsch, *Our Famous Guest*, p. 113.

17. "About Play-Acting" appeared in the October 1898 *Forum* and is reprinted in Twain, *The Man that Corrupted Hadleyburg and Other Stories and Essays* [1900] (New York: Oxford University Press, 1996), pp. 235–51.

18. Ludwig Eisenberg, *Das geistege Wien* (Vienna: C. Daberkow's Verlag, 1893), vol. 1, pp. 485–86, cited in Schirer, *Twain and the Theatre*, p. 96. Schirer translates this play's title as "Women in Politics." See also Dolmetsch, *Our Famous Guest*, pp. 121–25. For more on these proposed collaborations, see Schirer, *Twain and the Theatre*, pp. 95–97. Also Paine, *Biography*, vol. 2, p. 1075—although, as Dolmetsch notes, Paine misdates activities from the first winter in Vienna as having taken place during Twain's second winter there.

19. Clemens to Rogers, 15 March 1898, *Mark Twain's Correspondence with Henry Huttleston Rogers, 1893–1909*, ed. Lewis Leary (Berkeley: University of California Press, 1969), p. 326; Dolmetsch, *Our Famous Guest*, pp. 128–29.

20. Notebook 42 (June 1897–March 1900), typescript p. 52, in the Mark Twain Papers; also available in *Microfilm Edition of Mark Twain's Literary Manuscripts Available in the Mark Twain Papers*, vol. 33.

21. Notebook 42 (June 1897–March 1900), typescript p. 53, in the Mark Twain Papers; quoted in Dolmetsch, *Our Famous Guest*, p. 119. The notation "Vienna, Feb. 21, 1898" appears on the manuscript in Twain's handwriting, but Dolmetsch surmises that this is "presumably the date on which it was received from his copyist," since Twain's letter of 5 February 1898 to Henry Rogers (Leary, *Correspondence with Rogers*, p. 319) notes that Twain completed the play on February 5 (p. 333).

22. Mark Twain, *The Innocents Abroad* [1869] (New York: Oxford University Press, 1996), p. 288.

23. Ibid., p. 137.
24. Clemens to Joseph H. Twichell, 5 January 1874, Frank and Smith, *Twain's Letters*, vol. 6, p. 11; see also p. 12n3.
25. Mark Twain, *A Tramp Abroad* [1880] (New York: Oxford University Press, 1996), pp. 558–59.
26. Ibid., p. 560.
27. Ibid., p. 561.
28. Lawrence J. Oliver, "Art," LeMaster and Wilson, *Mark Twain Encyclopedia*, p. 40.
29. Twain, *A Tramp Abroad*, pp. 563–566.
30. *The New Metropolitan* (April 1903), p. 6. To see these images and for additional useful information about Twain's views on art, see "Mark Twain Takes on Art. Selections from an exhibition of Spring 2001 from the Mark Twain Papers at The Bancroft Library, University of California, Berkeley," curated by Lin Salamo with the assistance of Michael B. Frank and Anh Bui (available at http://Bancroft.Berkeley.edu/MTP/art.html). One can find additional, extended acerbic comments on art critics as well as intelligent discussions of art in the opening pages of Mark Twain's unpublished notebook from 1892 in the Harry Ransom Humanities Research Center, University of Texas at Austin (see Samuel L. Clemens, "Autograph Notebook with miscellaneous addresses and manuscripts" [1892], unpaginated).
31. Karl Gerhardt (1853–1940) was a young mechanic working at Pratt and Whitney in Hartford, Conn., with raw talent as a sculptor, whom Twain met in early 1881. Twain invited John Quincy Adams Ward, a sculptor who was president of the National Academy of Design, to evaluate Gerhardt's work. When Ward suggested that Gerhardt would benefit from study in Paris, Twain decided to subsidize that training himself and sent him to Europe (Clemens to Howells, 21 February 1881, Smith and Gibson, *Twain-Howells Letters*, vol. 1, pp. 350–55). Gerhardt returned to Hartford in 1884 and sculpted the bust of Twain that appears as the frontispiece in *Adventures of Huckleberry Finn*. He would later have commissions to sculpt Ulysses S. Grant and Henry Ward Beecher, among others.
32. It is unclear exactly how Charles Ethan Porter (1847?–1923) met Twain, but we know that he first came to Twain's attention in the late 1870s. Porter aspired to gain attention in the social circle in which Twain moved in Hartford; in addition, the fact that he was a black painter struggling against difficult odds is likely to have helped interest Twain in his case. As a contemporary art historian put it, "Being a colored man, Mr. Porter has found shameful obstacles placed in his path, but is manfully fighting them with a love of art and an enthusiasm that must conquer." H. W. French, *Art and Artists in Connecticut* (New York: Charles T. Dillingham, 1879), p. 160. Thomas Riggio believes that Porter and Twain may have met on May 29, 1880, when Twain acted as one of two auctioneers on the program of a charity event to which Porter had donated a piece of art. On November 7, 1881, Twain wrote to Gerhardt and his wife, Josephine, then living in Paris, asking them to help get Porter settled in that city. The letter "was meant to open doors for Porter in the select community of artists that Americans were eager to join in Paris." Thomas P. Riggio, "Charles Ethan Porter and Mark Twain," in *Charles Ethan Porter, 1847?–1923*, ed. Helen K. Fusscas (Marlborough: The Connecticut Gallery, 1987), p. 78. Porter's early landscape work got significant press attention in Hartford before he left for France, drawing positive comment from the artist Frederick Church in 1879, who said that Porter had "no superior as a colorist, in the United States"; Church bought some of Porter's paintings. Hildegard Cummings, "The

Hartford Artist," in Fusscas, *Porter*, p. 62. See also "An Artist Who Deserves Fame," *Hartford Evening Times*, 11 September 1879. Church, as it turns out, was the first painter to capture Twain's attention and interest, and Church's high opinion of Porter may well have encouraged Twain to support Porter's work. In St. Louis in 1861, when he was twenty-five and still two years away from assuming the pen name "Mark Twain," Clemens called Church's *Heart of the Andes*, a nearly ten-foot-wide panoramic canvas that had been exhibited before appreciative crowds in the United States and Britain since 1859, "the most wonderfully beautiful painting which this city has ever seen." Branch et al., *Twain's Letters*, vol. 1, p. 117. He and Church would later become friends. Porter left for Paris in November 1881, his trip subsidized in good part by Twain, and returned to Hartford in early 1884. Porter also contributed to early exhibitions of Hartford's Decorative Art Society, a women's organization in which Clemens's wife, Olivia Langdon Clemens, was active. Only one painting remains "that can be identified with certainty from the Paris years." Fusscas notes that "This painting indicates that Porter's art had not only been influenced by the new styles of Paris, it had been revolutionized by them" (Fusscas, *Porter*, p. 28). "The artist absorbed the new concepts prevailing in the French art world, particularly those of the Barbizon School" (Fusscas, *Porter*, p. 10). "The influence of the French Barbizon school of landscape must have been a very important factor in Porter's experience abroad. He went to Europe still determined to be a landscape painter. . . . He would have studied the reigning masters of French landscape on view in Paris. The Barbizon painters, who had all died in the previous ten years, were being honored and exhibited in many places. . . . Their interest in outdoor, simple landscape seen freshly and without a salon finish would have been sympathetic to Porter's own American Pre-Raphaelite vision. Furthermore, their paintings were avidly collected by American patrons" (Fusscas, *Porter*, p. 38). Later paintings by Porter were credited by newspapers with showing the influence of Barbizon School painters as well (Fusscas, *Porter*, pp. 10, 38). See also Robert L. Herbert, *Barbizon Revisited* (exhibition catalogue, Boston: Museum of Fine Arts, 1962).

33. Twain was an official witness at the 1879 wedding in Paris of Francis D. (Frank) Millet to Lily Merrell of Boston. LeMaster and Wilson, *Mark Twain Encyclopedia*, p. 514. In addition to painting, Frank Millet frequently wrote articles on art, such as F. D. Millet, "What Are Americans Doing in Art?" *Century Magazine* 43 (November 1891): 46. For other friendships with artists, see Clemens to Howells, 24 July 1889, Smith and Gibson, *Twain-Howells Letters*, vol. 2, pp. 607–8; and Clemens to Olivia Langdon Clemens, 27–30 January 1894 and 7 February 1894, Paine, *Twain's Letters*, vol. 2, pp. 603–9 (undated fragments). This series of late January and early February 1894 letters between Twain and his wife are dated and fully published in *Microfilm Edition of Mark Twain's Manuscript Letters Now in the Mark Twain Papers* (Berkeley: The Bancroft Library, 2002), vol. 7. Other artists with whom Twain was acquainted include Carroll Beckwith, E. A. Abbey, and Abbott H. Thayer. Paine, *Biography*, vol. 2, pp. 900, 901, 1062, 1104; vol. 3, p. 1237.

34. Elbert Hubbard, *Little Journeys to the Homes of Eminent Painters* (East Aurora, N.Y.: Roy Crofters, 1912), book 2, p. 85.

35. Although Millet disavowed any political intent, a critic in *Le Figaro* saw behind his painting *The Gleaners* ominous portents of potential violence: "Behind these three *Gleaners*, on the murky horizon, loom the rioters' pikes and the scaffolds of 1793." Quoted in Roseline

Bacou, *Millet: One Hundred Drawings*, trans. James Emmons (New York: Harper & Row, 1975), p. 12.

36. Julia Cartwright (Mrs. Henry Ady), *Jean François Millet: His Life and Letters* (London: Swann Sonnenschein, 1896, 1902; New York: Macmillan, 1910), pp. 370–371; Laura Meixner, "Jean-François Millet and his American Protégés," in *An International Episode: Millet, Monet and their North American Counterparts* (exhibition catalogue, Memphis: The Dixon Gallery and Gardens, 1982), pp. 14, 73. Many of the Millets in Shaw's collection would be exhibited at the Boston Athenaeum three months after Millet's death in 1875.

37. Edward Wheelwright, "Personal Recollections of Jean-François Millet," *Atlantic Monthly* 37, no. 227 (September 1876): 257–76; Meixner, "Millet and his American Protégés," p. 45; Wyatt Eaton, "Recollections of Jean François Millet," *Century Magazine*, 38, no. 1 (May 1889): 90–104; Will H. Low, "Jean Francois Millet," *McClure's Magazine* 7 (May 1896): 499–512; Susan Fleming, "The Boston Patrons of Jean-François Millet," in Alexandra Murphy, *Jean-François Millet* (exhibition catalogue, Boston: Museum of Fine Arts, 1984), p. ix. In addition to Shaw and Hunt, Martin Brimmer, first president of the Museum of Fine Arts, deserves credit for establishing Millet's reputation in Boston.

38. Fleming, "Boston Patrons of Millet," p. xv.

39. William Dean Howells, *The Coast of Bohemia* [1893] (New York: Harper & Brothers, 1901), p. 6.

40. Cartwright, *Millet*, pp. 370–71. For the ubiquity of reproductions of Millet's works during this era, see Michael Conforti, "Foreword," in Alexandra R. Murphy, Richard Rand, Brian T. Allen, James Ganz and Alexis Goodin, *Jean-François Millet: Drawn into the Light* (exhibition catalogue, Williamstown, Mass.: Sterling and Francine Clark Art Institute, 1999), p. vii.

41. In her 1977 work on Millet, Griselda Pollock explains that what was "dangerous and explosive in 1848 in the extreme turmoil of revolution, could become the supreme symbol of natural and eternal man . . . once the new order had emerged stable and triumphant." Pollock, *Millet* (London: Oresko Books, 1977), p. 8. Emerson quoted in F. O. Matthiessen, *American Renaissance* (New York: Oxford University Press, 1941), p. 39; Wheelright, "Personal Recollections of Millet," p. 206; Fleming, "Boston Patrons of Millet," pp. xv, xvii.

42. Whitman "considered Millet 'A whole religion in himself: The best of democracy, the best of all well-bottomed faith is in his pictures. The man who knows Millet needs no creed.'" He viewed his own *Leaves of Grass* as "Millet in another form." Quoted in Fleming, "Boston Patrons of Millet," p. xvii. See also Henry Childs Merwin, "Millet and Walt Whitman," *Atlantic Monthly* 79 (May 1897): 719–20.

43. Although Dolmetsch attributes this remark to Twain (*Our Famous Guest*, p. 144), Ossip Gabrilowitsch, who was present on the occasion the remark was made, recalls in an article he wrote in the *New York Times* in 1930 ("Memoirs of Leschetizky") that it was Leschetizky who said it. Article quoted in *Mark Twain's Notebook*, ed. Albert Bigelow Paine (New York: Harper & Brothers, 1935), p. 354.

44. Paine, *Biography*, vol. 2, p. 1062. In a journal entry, Twain conveys some of that variety: "May 9, '98, Vienna. Visitors yesterday, Countess Wydenbruck-Esterhazy, Austrian; Nansen & his wife, Norwegians; Freiherr ~~von~~ de Laszowski, Pole; his niece, Hungarian;

Madame ***, Hollander; 5 Americans & 3 other nationalities (French, German, English.) Certainly *there is plenty of variety in Vienna*" (emphasis in original), Notebook 40 (January 1897–July 1899), typescript p. 20, in the Mark Twain Papers; also available in *Microfilm Edition of Mark Twain's Literary Manuscripts Available in the Mark Twain Papers*, vol. 33. And if Vienna contributed a diverse international mix of artists to the brew, it may also have played a role in shaping the respect for friendship that runs through the play. Twain wrote Laurence Hutton on February 20, 1898, that "We all like Vienna. Among our numerous acquaintances we count several friends—friends whom we love and profoundly value. It is friends that make life." Leary, *Correspondence with Rogers*, p. 293.

45. Wheelright, "Personal Recollections of Millet," pp. 257–76; drawing, p. 261. A drawing of Millet's studio by Lyell Carr accompanied Wyatt Eaton's 1889 article in *Century Magazine*; the caption read: "Millet's Studio. From a photograph by Karl Bodmer made several years after Millet's death, giving a partial aspect of the studio as it was when occupied by Millet." Wyatt Eaton, "Recollections of Jean Francois Millet," *Century Magazine* 38, no. 1 (May 1889): 90–104; drawing, p. 95.

46. Justin Kaplan writes that Twain's "villains" during the bleak period of his bankruptcy were "[Typesetter inventor] Paige, [Twain's nephew and business manager] Charley Webster, various publishers, businessmen, bankers." Kaplan, *Mr. Clemens and Mark Twain: A Biography* (New York: Simon and Schuster, 1966), p. 344.

47. "Barbizon was, in fact, a prosperous place; there was no real poverty there," Edward Wheelwright had written in the *Atlantic Monthly* in 1876. Wheelwright, "Personal Recollections of Millet," p. 274. Twenty years later, T. H. Bartlett noted that "The peasants of Barbizon knew that [Millet] earned more money than all of them put together. . . .The Millets lived like generous Normands, their table was always bountifully spread, and their children were fed for health and good blood." Bartlett described "the immense dishes of meat and vegetables that loaded their table and filled the whole house with their nourishing smell." T. H. Bartlett, "Barbizon and Jean-François Millet," *Scribner's Magazine* 7, no. 5 (May 1890): 553.

48. Alfred Sensier, *Jean-François Millet, paysan et peintre* [1881], p. xi; quoted in Griselda Pollock, *Millet* (London: Oresko Books, 1977), p. 5. Sensier's book was originally published under the title *La Vie et L'oeuvre de J.F. Millet. Par Alfred Sensier.* Manuscrit publié par Paul Mantz. Avec de nombreux facsimile (Paris: A. Quantin. New York: J. W. Bouton, 1881).

49. "Every body was going to the famous Paris Exposition—I, too was going to the Paris Exposition," Twain writes near the start of *Innocents Abroad*, noting the Exposition-fever that seemed to have gripped his countrymen in 1867. Twain, *Innocents Abroad*, p. 27. Paintings exhibited there by Millet included *Les Glaneuses, La Jeune Bergère, La Grande Tondeuse, Le Berger, Les Planteur de Pommes de Terre, Le Parc aux Moutons, La Récolte de Pommes de Terre*, as well as the *Angelus* (Cartwright, *Millet*, p. 297).

50. "Jean-François Millet," *New York Times*, 17 February 1875, quoted in Laura Meixner, "The 'Millet Myth' and the American Public," in *An International Episode: Millet, Monet and their North American Counterparts* (exhibition catalogue, Memphis: The Dixon Gallery and Gardens, 1982). Other articles on Millet's death appeared in the *New York Times* on the following dates: 7 February 1875, p. 17; 9 February 1875, p. 7; 21 February 1875, p. 8; see also "Jean Francois Millet," *New York Times*, 18 April 1875, p. 4.

51. "The Quincy Adams Shaw Collection at the Athenaeum," *Boston Daily Advertiser*, 5 May 1875; Charles H. Moore, "The Marriage of St. Catherine," *Boston Daily Advertiser*, 2 June 1875; William Morris Hunt, "Art," *Boston Daily Advertiser*, 9 June 1875; "French Art," *Boston Daily Advertiser*, 11 June 1875; Henry James, "Art," *Nation* 20 (June 1875): 410; "Art," *Atlantic Monthly* 36 (September 1875): 374–75; Meixner, "Millet Myth," pp. 74–75.

52. Wheelwright, "Personal Recollections of Millet," pp. 257, 260, 261. In this article, which appeared the same year Twain published *Tom Sawyer*, Wheelwright referred to Millet's paintings as "hymns" the artist had "written on canvas" (p. 275). It is interesting that Twain used the word "hymn" in an analogous metaphor when he referred to his novel *Tom Sawyer* as "simply a hymn, put into prose form to give it a worldly air." Unmailed answer to a correspondent, 8 September 1887, Paine, *Twain's Letters*, vol. 2, p. 477.

53. Twain wrote Howells that Howells's play *The Parlor Car* "is perfect, in the magazine," the same month that the play appeared in the *Atlantic Monthly*. Clemens to Howells, 14 September 1876, Smith and Gibson, *Twain-Howells Letters*, vol. 1, p. 152. Twain himself contributed two pieces to the magazine that fall and had published his "Old Times on the Mississippi" in it the previous year.

54. Helena De Kay's translation of Alfred Sensier, *La Vie et L'Oeuvre de Jean-François Millet*, retitled *Jean-François Millet: Peasant and Painter* (Boston: James R. Osgood, 1881) was originally serialized in *Scribner's Monthly Magazine* in 1880 (vol. 20, no. 5, pp. 732–50 and no. 6, pp. 825–40; vol. 21, no. 1, pp. 104–10 and no. 2, pp. 189–200). A review of De Kay's translation of Sensier appeared 23 January 1881 in the *New York Tribune* (p. 8). Other reviews include W. C. Brownell, "Sensier's Life of Jean Francois Millet," *Nation* 32 (1881): 116; and "Millet, Peasant and Painter," *New York Times*, 22 December 1880, p. 3. De Kay's translation of Sensier was all the more noteworthy for being the earliest English translation available in the United States of a biography of a Barbizon artist. See "Millet's Home Life. Notes of a Visit to the Artist at Barbizon," *New York Tribune*, 8 December 1889, p. 15. Twain took the river trip with Osgood to research *Life on the Mississippi*, which Osgood published in 1883.

55. Meixner, "Millet Myth," pp. 68, 76. Robert Herbert, "Millet Revisited," *Burlington Magazine* 104 (September 1962): 294–305.

56. Quoted in Meixner, "Millet Myth," p. 76.

57. Ibid.

58. Ibid., pp. 76, 83. See, for example, G. R. Tomson's villanelle, "Jean-François Millet," *Atlantic Monthly* 60, no. 358 (August 1887): 186.

59. Wyatt Eaton, "Recollections of Jean François Millet," *Century Magazine* 38, no. 1 (May 1889): 90–104.

60. Theodore Child, "Jean François Millet: The Millet Exhibition in Paris," *Atlantic Monthly* 60 (October 1887): 506–15; W. C. Brownell, "Sensier's Life of Jean Francois Millet," *Nation* 32 (1881): 116; J. J. Jarves, "Millet's Pictures; Increased Value of," *New York Times*, 4 May 1881, p. 2; "Jean Francois Millet," *New York Tribune*, 23 January 1881, p. 8; "Millet's House Pulled Down," *New York Tribune*, 17 October 1889, p. 7; "Millet's Home Life," *New York Tribune*, 8 December 1889, p. 15; "Millet, Francois, and the 'Angelus,'" *New York Tribune*, 22 July 1889, p. 5.

61. The passages quoted here come from Julia (Cartwright) Ady, "Jean-François Millet," *Nine-*

teenth Century 24 (September 1888): 419, 434. Twain's familiarity with this journal during this period is noted in Alan Gribben, *Mark Twain's Library: A Reconstruction,* vol. 2 (Boston: G. K. Hall, 1980), p. 509. (Gribben's two-volume reference work on Mark Twain's reading is a useful source generally for determining his familiarity with newspapers and periodicals, and has been helpful in determining the likelihood that Twain would have seen many of the articles mentioned in this section.) One might note that journalists did not unanimously endorse the "Millet myth." Also in 1889, for example, the *New York Tribune* reprinted an article from the London *Globe* (that had described Millet as having been relatively comfortable from a financial standpoint) and referred to "the famous legend of the misery which enveloped and at the same time strangled the great painter and his family" ("Millet and 'The Angelus.' The Painter's Life—Gambetta's Views of Art. From the London Globe," *New York Tribune,* 22 July 1889, p. 5). The "Millet myth" was also referred to by that name in an article in December 1889 in the *New York Tribune,* which criticized the "persistent gloom" of Sensier's biography and noted that Millet's affairs had been "comparatively prosperous" ("Millet's Home Life. Notes of a Visit to the Artist at Barbizon," *New York Tribune,* 8 December 1889, p. 5).

62. "Millet's Great Work. History of the Painting Which Brought So Great a Price," *New York Times,* 3 July 1889, p. 2.

63. Cartwright, *Millet,* p. 366. (This is not a complete list of parties who owned the painting during this period.)

64. "At the Secrétan Sale. Scenes and Incidents of the Great Occasion," *New York Times,* 14 July 1889, p. 5. According to an article (datelined "Paris, July 16") that appeared in the London *Times* (17 July 1889, p. 5), Proust had twenty-seven associates involved in his bid, a group that included "Frenchman, Russians, and Danes." For account of Proust's bid in dollars, see "Secrétan's Great Sale. Scattering His Many Art Treasures. Millet's 'L'Angelus' Going to the Louvre for $111,000," *New York Times,* 2 July 1889, p. 1. The Americans paid an unheard-of 580,650 francs (the painting's sale price is reported in several sources, including the London *Times,* 3 August 1889, p. 5). In the play, when Twain refers to "The sale of the 'Angelus' by auction, to an American for 500,000 francs and France's re-purchase of it on the spot for 550,000," he is not quite accurate, seemingly conflating the two auctions involving Secrétan, one in 1881, the other in 1889; nonetheless Twain conveys the general spirit of what transpired. See, for example, Cartwright, *Millet,* pp. 365–69, and Meixner, "Millet and his American Protégés," pp. 81–82.

65. "Editor's Easy Chair," *Harper's* 80, no. 479 (April 1890): 800–801. See also "Art—Millet's 'Angelus,'" *New York Times,* 25 October 1889, p. 8. The exhibit was to raise funds for a monument to artist Antoine-Louis Barye, best known for his sculptures. But Millet's painting received the lion's share of the press coverage of the exhibit, along with the work of Barye. (The exhibit also included work by Jean-Baptiste-Camille Corot, Eugène Delacroix, Théodore Géricault, Henri Rousseau, Constant Troyon, and others.) See, for example, "Art of Brush and Chisel. Loans in Honor of Barye, the Sculptor. 'The Angelus' and Other Masterpieces of French Painting Shown with Hundreds of Bronzes," *New York Times,* 16 November 1889, p. 5. This article notes that "'The Angelus' is naturally the great point of attraction. . . . There may be other Millets as fine, or even finer, according to different tastes. But there is but one 'Angelus' and Millet was its maker."

66. Articles published in the 1890s about Millet include the following: P. Millet, "Poverty and Insanity," *New York Times,* 1 August 1891, p. 2; Charles De Kay, "Millet's Barbizon House and Life Described by C. de Kay," *New York Times,* 9 August, 1891, p. 1; Charles De Kay, "Caen-Barbizon; Millet, Diaz, and Rousseau's Houses," Letter to the *New York Times,* 9 August 1891, p. 12 (Charles De Kay was a contributor to the *Atlantic Monthly*). Years earlier Twain had referred to a piece by him in the magazine in a letter to Howells. Twain to Howells, 11 January 1876, Smith and Gibson, *Twain-Howells Letters,* pp. 119–120; V. Verestchagin, "Millet's 'Angelus' Fraudulent Sales Scandal Explained—Editorial," *New York Times,* 27 December 1891, p. 4; "No Fury Like an Artist Scorned," *New York Times,* 27 December 1891, p. 4; "London, England. Art; Royal Academy; Election-Royal Academy Exhibition; Paintings by Bridgman, Boughton, and Millet Criticised," *New York Times,* 29 April 1892, p. 19; 30 April 1892, p. 5; and 1 May 1892, pp. 2–3; W. C. Larned, "Millet and Recent Criticism," *Scribner's Magazine* 8, no. 3 (September 1890): 390–92; T. H. Bartlett, "Barbizon and Jean François Millet," *Scribner's Magazine* 7, no. 5 (May 1890): 530–55; T. H. Bartlett, "Barbizon and Jean-François Millet" (Part 2), *Scribner's Magazine* 7, no. 6 (June 1890): 735–55; Pierre Millet, "The Story of Millet's Early Life, Told by His Younger Brother," *The Century* 45, no. 3 (January 1893): 380–86; Pierre Millet, "'Millet's Life at Barbizon.' Described by His Younger Brother," *Century Illustrated Magazine* 47, no. 6 (April 1894): 908–15; "Work of Jean Francois Millet," *Saturday Review of Politics, Literature, Science and Art* 79 (1895): 98. See also Edward Carpenter, "Wagner, Millet and Whitman—in Relation to Art and Democracy," *Progressive Review* 1 (October 1896): 63. Also [Review of Cartwright biography], *Review of Reviews* (London edition) 14 (October 1896): 318; [Review of Cartwright biography], *New York Times,* 17 October 1896, p. 3; "Cartwright's Life and Letters," *Westminster Review* (December 1896), p. 713; "Fine Arts. Rev. of Jean Francois Millet. His Life and Letters by Julia Cartwright. Illustrated," *Athenaeum* no. 3643 (21 August 1897): 264–65; Will H. Low, "Jean Francois Millet," *McClure's Magazine* 6 (May 1896): 499; Henry Childs Merwin, "Millet and Walt Whitman," *Atlantic* 79 (May 1897): 719–20. See also Sidney Thompson, "Millet's Barbizon," *Leslie's Illustrated Weekly* 85 (20 September 1897): 218.

67. Salvador Dalí, *Le mythe tragique de l'Angelus de Millet* (Paris: J.-J. Pauvert, 1963), pp. 7–9 (the book was written in 1932 but not published until 1963); see particularly p. 8, for "Radiographie de la partie inférieure de L'Angélus, exécutée dans le laboratoire du Musée du Louvre à la demande de Salvador Dalí." See also Salvador Dalí, *The Tragic Myth of Millet's Angelus: Paranoiac-critical Interpretation Including the Myth of William Tell,* trans. Eleanor R. Morse, ed. A. Reynolds Morse (St. Petersburg, Fla.: Salvador Dalí Museum, 1986); Dawn Ades and Fiona Bradley, "Introduction," *Salvador Dalí: A Mythology* (London: Tate Gallery Publishing, 1998), p. 9; Fiona Bradley, "Dalí as Myth-Maker: The Tragic Myth of Millet's Angelus," in Ades and Bradley, *Salvador Dalí: A Mythology,* pp. 12, 14–16, 18.

68. "Angelus" [entry], *The HarperCollins Encyclopedia of Catholicism* (San Francisco: Harper-Collins, 1995), p. 48; "Angelus" [entry], John A. Hardon, S.J., *Modern Catholic Dictionary* (Garden City, N.Y.: Doubleday, 1980). "Angelus" [entry], *The New Catholic Encyclopedia* (New York: The McGraw-Hill Book Company, 1967). None of these encyclopedia entries associate the prayer with memorializing loved ones. Millet's reminiscence about his grandmother is quoted in Pollock, *Millet,* p. 18.

69. Mark Twain, "Is He Living or Is He Dead?" [1893], in *Man that Corrupted Hadleyburg*, pp. 183–86, 188.

70. "Dialogue is the yeast that lightens the bread; & should be paid for at double rate—whereas by the word-system it counts the same as the dough," Twain complained to his friend Richard Watson Gilder, editor of the *Century Magazine*, in the spring of 1898. "Dialogue costs twice as much time & thought & emendation as does solid matter, & when satisfactorily done will hold a reader when solid matter won't." Clemens to Richard Watson Gilder, 29 April 1898, in Pierpont Morgan Library, New York; published in *Microfilm Edition of Mark Twain's Previously Unpublished Letters*, vol. 5. Twain's dialogue in *Is He Dead?* is brisk and colloquial, demonstrating his familiarity with a broad range of contemporary slang, such as Chicago's use of the word "spouted" for "pawned" in act 1, when he says "I . . . spouted my coat and vest and necktie" (Robert H. Hirst, personal communication, 12 February 2003).

71. Isoo Yamagata, trans., "Seishi Ikan" ("Is He Living or Is He Dead"), *Shonen Bunko* (November 1893), pp. 250–58. There is no record of any work by Twain being translated into Japanese and published before this one. Twain was thus introduced to Japan as the author of "Is He Living or Is He Dead?" Japanese translations of *Tom Sawyer* and *Huckleberry Finn* were published in 1919 and 1921, respectively. *Shonen Bunko*, the publication where the story first appeared, was a juvenile magazine. The translator, Isoo Yamagata, was a very well-known journalist. The story was translated again in 1916 by the prominent writer Kuni Sasaki, who included it in a book called *Yumoa Jippen* (Ten works of humor), a collection of Japanese translations of ten short stories by Mark Twain. Tsuyoshi Ishihara notes that although Twain's story was available in Japanese from 1893 on, it is possible that Takeo Arishima (1878–1923) read it in English during his studies in the United States from 1903 to around 1907 (Ishihara, personal communication, 17 January 2003).

72. There were other changes, as well. In an interesting twist, the plot of faking the artist's death is the brainchild of a female character, Tomoko, an artist's model who is both independent-minded and resourceful and who selects the "dead" artist as her mate—a twist not unexpected, perhaps, by a writer who pioneered in depicting the "New Woman" in Japanese literature. Arishima's play ends with the young artists informing art merchants of Domomata's death. It is unclear whether their plan will succeed or not (Ishihara, personal communication, 9 February 2002).

73. Takeo Arishima, *Domomata no Shi* (The death of Domomata), *Izumi* 1, no. 1 (Tokyo: Sobunkaku, 1922): 5–41; *Arishima Takeo Chosakushu* (The collected works of Arishima), vol. 16 (Tokyo: Sobunkaku, 1923), pp. 1–52.

74. Tsuyoshi Ishihara observes that although Japanese adaptations of *Huckleberry Finn*, *Tom Sawyer*, and *The Prince and the Pauper* are more familiar to ordinary Japanese readers than Arishima's adaptation of "Is He Living or Is He Dead?" for Japanese scholars, Arishima's play is the best-known literary adaptation of any of Mark Twain's works. For an insightful discussion of Japanese adaptations of other works by Twain, see Tsuyoshi Ishihara, "Mark Twain in Japan: Mark Twain's Literature and 20th Century Japanese Popular Culture and Juvenile Literature" (Ph.D. diss., University of Texas, Department of American Studies, 2003). Arishima's play was the subject of so many scholarly articles in Japan that Shunsuke Kamei and Yoshio Katsuura, two of the twentieth century's leading Japanese

Twain scholars, felt compelled to refrain from discussing it in any detail in their major books and essays on Twain and Japan in order to focus instead on less well-known adaptations. Yoshio Katsuura, *Nihon ni Okeru Mark Twain: Gaisetsu to Bunken Mokuroku* (Mark Twain in Japan: survey and bibliography) (Tokyo: Kirihara Shoten, 1979), p. 88; Shunsuke Kamei, "Hikaku Bungaku: Nihon ni okeru Maku Toein" ("Comparative literature: Mark Twain in Japan"), in *Koza Hikaku Bunka: Hikaku Bunka he no Tenbo* (Comparative perspectives on culture), ed. Shuntaro Ito (Tokyo: Kenkyusha, 1977), pp. 193–94; Arishima's adaptation is also mentioned briefly in Shunsuke Kamei, "Mark Twain in Japan, Reconsidered," in *Crosscurrents in the Literatures of Asia and the West*, ed. Masayuki Akiyama and Yiu-nam Leung (Newark, N.J.: University of Delaware Press, 1997), pp. 75–76. In this last essay (which was written in English) Kamei observed that "the hilarious vitality that abounds in Twain's story was lost" in Arishima's adaptation, "and the sentimental friendship and simple antiphilistinism of the young artists were emphasized" (pp. 75–76). Scholarly articles about Arishima's dramatic adaptation of "Is He Living or Is He Dead?" include the following: Saburo Ota, "Mark Twain to Arishima Takeo: *Domomata no Shi* wo meguru Mondai" ("Mark Twain and Takeo Arishima: issues around 'The Death of Domomata.'"), Showa Women's College Eibei Bungaku Kiyo, *Gakuen* 4 (1962): 22–36; Saburo Ota, "Arishima Takeo, *Domomata no Shi*" ("Takeo Arishima, 'The Death of Domomata'") in Saburo Ota, *Kindai Sakka to Seiyo* (Modern writer and the West) (Tokyo: Shimizu Kobundo, 1977), 66–91; Yoshitaka Yoshitake, "Arishima Takeo no Hon'angeki *Domomata no Shi*" ("Takeo Arishima's play adaptation, 'The Death of Domomata'"), in *Kindai Bungaku no Naka no Seiyo* (Western Europe in modern literature) by Yoshitaka Yoshitake (Tokyo: Kyoiku Shuppan Center, 1974), pp. 245–52; Fumiko Torii, "Arishima Takeo *Domomata no Shi* ni tsuite" ("On Takeo Arishima's 'The Death of Domomata'"), *Jissen Bungaku* 10 (1960): 4–8; Saeko Suzuki, "Arishima Takeo *Domomata no Shi* no Buntai to Kosei: Mark Twain to no Kankei ni tsuite" (The style and structure of Takeo Arishima's 'The Death of Domomata': comparison with Mark Twain"), *Jissen Kokubungaku* 26 (1984): 55–65 (Ishihara, personal communication, spring 2002–spring 2003).

75. The play was performed on November 23, 1922 at Toyo University Auditorium (Tokyo) and on December 23–24, 1922 by Shingekiza theater group, in Hochi Auditorium (Tokyo), directed by Ochiai Namio (Ishihara, personal communication, 18 January 2003). For more on Arishima, see Leith Morton, *Divided Self: A Biography of Arishima Takeo* (North Sydney, Australia: Allen & Unwin, 1988).

76. "The Legend of the Capitoline Venus" first appeared in the *Buffalo Express*, 23 October 1869. It may be found in *Sketches, New and Old* [1875] (New York: Oxford University Press, 1996), pp. 222–28 (the original title is kept in the table of contents but the story is titled "The Capitoline Venus" in the text). The story has its roots in a conversation with a guide that Twain reported several years earlier in *Innocents Abroad* (p. 20).

77. Twain, "The Capitoline Venus," p. 226.

78. Mark Twain first published "An Encounter With an Interviewer" in *Lotos Leaves*, ed. John Brougham and John Elderkin (Boston: William F. Gill, 1875), issued in November 1874. It may be found in *Mark Twain: Collected Tales, Sketches, Speeches, & Essays, 1852–1890*, ed. Louis J. Budd (New York: Library of America, 1992), pp. 583–87.

79. Ibid., pp. 585–86.

80. Twain more frequently wrote about cross-dressing women. For a helpful analysis of his "transvestite tales" see Susan Gillman, *Dark Twins: Imposture and Identity in Mark Twain's America* (Chicago: University of Chicago Press, 1989), pp. 96–135. See also Laura Skandera-Trombley, "Mark Twain's Cross-Dressing Oeuvre," *College Literature* 24, no. 2 (June 1997): 82–96. Twain's "An Awful—Terrible Medieval Romance," which appeared in 1870 in the *Buffalo Express* (and was reprinted as "A Medieval Romance," in *Sketches, New and Old*) featured both a male and a female who, for complicated political reasons, were forced to live out their lives as transvestites and who married each other as adults. The story was a parody of the hopelessly trite and formulaic romantic drivel that infuriated Twain. Unlike the authors of ponderous and contrived plots whom he ridiculed, Twain claimed that he did not know how to end his story: "The truth is, I have got my hero (or heroine) into such a particularly close place that I do not see how I am ever going to get him (or her) out of it again, and therefore I will wash my hands of the whole business. . . . I thought it was going to be easy enough to straighten out that little difficulty, but it looks different now." Twain, "A Medieval Romance," in *Sketches, New and Old*, p. 179. Some twenty years later, when he wrote *Is He Dead?* Twain might have found it just as tricky to extricate Millet from the "close place" he had gotten him into, what with Marie convinced he was dead and André determined to marry him. But, in *Is He Dead?* by crafting a memorable scene that gives fresh meaning to the idea of the "construction of gender," Twain found a way of moving beyond the impasse.

81. The short story "Wapping Alice" is reprinted in Mark Twain, *How Nancy Jackson Married Kate Wilson and Other Tales of Rebellious Girls & Daring Young Women*, ed. John Cooley (Lincoln: University of Nebraska Press, 2001), pp. 81–104.

82. Gillman, *Dark Twins*, p. 125.

83. Mark Twain, *The Tragedy of Pudd'nhead Wilson and the Comedy, Those Extraordinary Twins* [1894] (New York: Oxford University Press, 1996), pp. 41–49.

84. Sellers also speaks an early variant of what will become one of Chicago's most-repeated lines. Sellers says, "Cheer up, old friend, cheer up. Things are not so bad as they seem," while Chicago says, "Cheer up—cheer up—the worst is yet to come!" five times in *Is He Dead?* Colonel Sellers's line is from act 5, scene 1. This is the same line Twain wrote his wife when he declared bankruptcy, as is noted below.

85. Mark Twain, *Following the Equator* [1897] (New York: Oxford University Press, 1996), p. 413.

86. Ibid., p. 414.

87. R. Kent Rasmussen, *Mark Twain A to Z* (New York: Oxford University Press, 1995), p. 247.

88. Critics Steven E. Kemper and Forrest G. Robinson read the story, with its "humorous management of suspense" and "tone of mock ghoulishness," as a parody of themes and techniques used in tales by Edgar Allan Poe. Steven F. Kemper, "Poe, Twain, and Limburger Cheese," *Mark Twain Journal* 21 (1981): 13–14; Forrest G. Robinson, "Afterword," in Mark Twain, *Merry Tales* [1892] (New York: Oxford University Press, 1996), pp. 4–5.

89. Anne Bernays, "Introduction," in *Merry Tales*, p. xl.

90. Mark Twain, "Invalid's Story," in *Merry Tales*, p. 53.

91. "Whereas" appeared in the *Californian*, 22 October 1864. It may be found under the title "Aurelia's Unfortunate Young Man" in Twain, *Sketches, New and Old*, pp. 253–56.

92. Mark Twain, *Roughing It* [1872] (New York: Oxford University Press, 1996), pp. 384–86.

93. Twain, "The Lowest Animal" [1897], in Mark Twain, *Letters from the Earth*, ed. Bernard De-Voto (New York: Harper & Row, 1962), p. 231.

94. Browning, Frank, and Salamo, *Twain's Notebooks & Journals*, vol. 3, p. 627n197. This note also observes that Cornbury Tillou is fictionalized as the kindhearted blacksmith "old Mr. Ballou" in chaps. 27–33 of *Roughing It*.

95. Mark Twain, *Life on the Mississippi* [1883] (New York: Oxford University Press, 1996), pp. 533–37. Twain mentioned Bismarck in journal entries in 1891, 1892, and 1898. See Browning, Frank, and Salamo, *Twain's Notebooks & Journals*, vol. 3, p. 616; Clemens, "Autograph Notebook" [1892], in Harry Ransom Humanities Research Center; and 7 August 1898, Notebook 42 (June 1897–March 1900), typescript p. 28, in the Mark Twain Papers; also available in *Microfilm Edition of Mark Twain's Literary Manuscripts Available in the Mark Twain Papers*, vol. 33. Twain also mentioned Bismarck in a letter to Rogers shortly after Bismarck's death. Clemens to Rogers, 3 August 1898, Leary, *Correspondence with Rogers*, p. 355.

96. Clemens to Olivia Langdon Clemens, 19 April 1894, quoted in Kaplan, *Mr. Clemens and Mark Twain*, p. 329. Twain actually wrote the line two years earlier in a stand-alone journal entry in 1892 (Clemens, "Autograph Notebook" [1892], in Harry Ransom Humanities Research Center).

97. Twain, *Innocents Abroad*, p. 292.

98. Peter Messent notes that Twain comments on the case directly on four occasions in *The Man That Corrupted Hadleyburg*, pp. 144–46, 170, 270, and 388–89. Messent writes, "Clearly Twain was both angered and intrigued by the case and was aware of its wider significance. So even a story like 'The Man That Corrupted Hadleyburg' itself, which nowhere mentions Dreyfus (but which was written in Vienna in 1898, the same year Zola published 'J'accuse'), should be read in its context." Peter Messent, *The Short Works of Mark Twain: A Critical Study* (Philadelphia: University of Pennsylvania Press, 2001), p. 161.

99. Clemens to Chatto and Windus, 8 February 1898, in Alderman Library, University of Virginia; and Clemens to J. Henry Harper, 8 February 1898, in Rare Book and Special Collections Library, University of Illinois. Both letters are published in *Microfilm Edition of Mark Twain's Previously Unpublished Letters*, vol. 5. See also "From the 'London Times' of 1904," a story Twain published in *Century Magazine* in 1898 satirizing the second Dreyfus trial. The story may be found in Budd, *Collected Tales, Sketches, Speeches, & Essays, 1891–1910*, pp. 273–83.

100. See Notebook 36 (December 1895–March 1896), typescript p. 39, in the Mark Twain Papers; also available in *Microfilm Edition of Mark Twain's Literary Manuscripts Available in the Mark Twain Papers*, vol. 33.

101. Clemens to Rogers, 20 January 1898, Leary, *Correspondence with Rogers*, p. 316.

102. Twain, "Concerning the Jews," in *The Man that Corrupted Hadleyburg*, p. 254; Twain, "From the 'London Times' of 1904," in *The Man that Corrupted Hadleyburg*, p. 146; Twain, "My First Lie and How I Got Out Of It" (initially published in the *New York World*, 10 December 1899), in *The Man that Corrupted Hadleyburg*, p. 170. Twain also attacked anti-Semitism in contexts outside of the Dreyfus affair. His most concentrated and best-known effort to examine and challenge anti-Semitism is his essay "Concerning the Jews," which he initially published in *Harper's Magazine* in 1899 and later included in revised form in *The*

Man that Corrupted Hadleyburg (pp. 252–83). Also noteworthy are two stories (or rather, two versions of one story) that Twain wrote in the 1890s but which were not published until after his death: "Randall's Jew Story" and "Newhouse's Jew Story." Both stories narrate an incident in which the generosity, courage, bravery, altruism, and wisdom of a Jewish passenger on a riverboat lead a bank president in one version or a riverboat pilot in the other (each of whom admits to having been an anti-Semite at the time this incident happened) to forbid any anti-Semitic comments in his presence for the rest of his life. See "Randall's Jew Story," in *Mark Twain's Fables of Man*, ed. John S. Tuckey (Berkeley: University of California Press, 1972), pp. 283–89; "Newhouse's Jew Story," in Tuckey, *Twain's Fables of Man*, pp. 279–82; Mark Twain, "My First Lie and How I Got Out of It," in *The Man that Corrupted Hadleyburg*, p. 170. Twain wrote this comment on Zola in his notebook on 1 December 1898 (Paine, *Mark Twain's Notebook*, p. 342). He sent the identical comment to the *New York Herald*, and it appeared in the Paris edition of that paper on 30 January 1898. Jim Zwick's comments on Zola and Twain's anti-imperialist writings may be found at http://www.boondocksnet.com/twainwww/essays/twain_dreyfus0005.html.

103. Twain, "Concerning the Jews," in *The Man that Corrupted Hadleyburg*, pp. 253–54.
104. Twain, *Innocents Abroad*, pp. 104, 106–7, 108–9, 136, 147, 153.
105. Rasmussen, *Mark Twain A to Z*, p. 156.
106. *Twain's Notebooks & Journals, Volume 2 (1877–1883)*, ed. Frederick Anderson, Lin Salamo, and Bernard L. Stein (Berkeley: University of California Press, 1975), pp. 220, 318, 320, 322–23. See also Twain, "The French and the Commanches," in *Letters from the Earth*, pp. 183–89.
107. Twain, *Sketches, New and Old*, p. 28.
108. Ironically, despite Twain's conviction that the French had no appreciation of or understanding of his own art, it was a French scholar who wrote the most important early study of critical and popular responses to Twain's writings after his death. See Roger Asselineau, *The Literary Reputation of Mark Twain from 1910 to 1950* (Paris: Didier, 1954).
109. See, for example, *Dutchman in London*, or *The Dutchman's Wife*, vaudeville scripts in the Tony Pastor vaudeville collection in the Harry Ransom Humanities Research Center at the University of Texas at Austin. The Dutchman in *Dutchman in London* says, "Vell I vas come by Englant at last. Mein Gott in Hummel. How I vas knocked about by dat ship. . . . I vas so sick mit mineself. I tought I vould got shipwrecked ven de ship was sticked in dat frog for two days un twenty six hours . . . " (p. 1). The Dutchman in *The Dutchman's Wife* says, "Vot is de matter of you can't attend by your business" (p. 1) or "Vell I bedam dat vas de funniest flying vot I never don't see before" (p. 1). Tony Pastor, often referred to as the father of vaudeville, presented shows like these at popular New York theatres from the 1880s through 1908. Pastor's Fourteenth Street Theatre was known for producing tasteful, clean shows suitable as family fare. In a vaudeville script quoted by Douglas Gilbert in *American Vaudeville*, a "Dutch" character says, "Py chimminy," while Twain's "Dutchy" says, "Py chorge." Douglas Gilbert, *American Vaudeville, Its Life and Time* (New York: McGraw-Hill, 1940), pp. 74–75. "Dutch" vaudeville acts grew extremely popular in the 1880s. One of the most famous was the low-comedy team of Joe Weber and Lew Fields, which got its start in Boston. Weber and Fields portrayed "Dutch"-dialect-speaking comic characters whose accents prevented them from understanding each other. Gavin Jones,

in his *Strange Talk: The Politics of Dialect Literature in Gilded Age America* (Berkeley: University of California Press, 1999), p. 168, quotes the following Weber and Fields routine (in which they play two characters named Mike and Meyer):

MEYER: Vot are you doing?
MIKE: Voiking in a nut factory.
MEYER: Doing vot?
MIKE: Nutting.
MEYER: Sure—but vot are you doing?
MIKE: Nutting
MEYER: I know, but vot voik are you going?
MIKE: Nutting, I tole you.
MEYER: *(Poking his finger in Mike's eye):* Ou-u-u-u, how I lofe you!

Meyer's "how I lofe you!" performs a bit of the same function as Dutchy's oft-repeated affectionate and admiring effusion—"Oh, dot Shecaggo!"—in *Is He Dead?*

110. The Garrick Theatre on West 35th Street was built by Edward ("Ned") Harrigan, who starred there in musicals he produced between 1890 and 1893 in which dialect humor was always central and often involved Irish and German characters. For more on Twain's attendance at one of Harrigan's shows in 1893, see Clemens to Olivia Langdon Clemens, 13 September 1893, *The Love Letters of Mark Twain*, ed. Dixon Wecter (New York: Harper & Brothers, 1949), p. 269.

111. For example, O'Shaughnessy says, "It's me trade" and "on me honor," while a Tim O'Hatch in Tony Pastor's *The Dutchman's Wife* says "I say me lad . . . " (p. 6). For more on the performance of Irish ethnicity on the Chautauqua circuit, see Marian Scott, *Chautauqua Caravan* (New York: Appleton, 1929).

112. Joseph Herbert's *The Geezer* was produced by Weber and Fields (1895 typescript, pp. 2, 4, 10, in the Harvard Theatre Collection; quotes used by courtesy of the Harvard Theatre Collection). Li-Hung-Chang's dialect is also reminiscent of that spoken by the title character in the play Twain coauthored with Bret Harte in 1877, *Ah Sin.*

113. Jones's comment from *Strange Talk*, p. 175.

114. The real Li Hung-chang (1823–1901) was viceroy of the capital province of Zhili for twenty-five years (1870–1895). He controlled foreign affairs for the Empress Dowager Tzu Hsi and was the chief negotiator of the 1895 treaty that ended the first Sino-Japanese War and of the 1896 treaty that allowed Russia to build the Trans-Siberian railroad across Manchuria. Later, in 1900, as viceroy of Guanzhou, he protected foreigners during the Boxer Rebellion. Twain was certainly aware of him by the fall of 1889, if not earlier. When the future of the Chinese Educational Mission in Hartford was in jeopardy in 1880, Twain's friend Rev. Joe Twichell, who had a strong personal interest in the survival of the mission, recalled both the honors Li Hung-chang had bestowed on Ulysses S. Grant when Grant had visited China and Grant's admiration of Mark Twain. Twichell persuaded Twain to visit the former president in New York that fall (not long after Twain had hosted Grant in Hartford) to join him in making a pitch for the Hartford mission. Twain obliged. A spirited discussion of China transpired at the meeting, and at the end, Twichell writes,

Grant "proposed, of his own accord, to write a letter to Li Hung Chang, advising the continuance of the Mission." Paine, *Biography*, vol. 2, pp. 694–95.

115. Li Hung Chang in *The Geezer*, for example, enters singing "I am Li Hung Chang / Let the cymbals clang / For you don't care a hang who I am; / There's no potentate / Either small or great / That can stop my gait / So salaam" (Herbert, *The Geezer*, p. 5).

116. W. C. Robey, *Li Hung Chang's Reception, A Burlesque Comedy in 1 Act*, Rare Book and Special Collections Division, Library of Congress (http://memory.loc.gov). Li Hung Chang speaks Standard English in both of these scripts rather than the stage-Chinese dialect spoken by the character Two-Hi in *The Geezer*. The Harvard typescript of *The Geezer* indicates that *"Li Hung Chang* was played by an *Irish Comedian* who made up exactly like Li Hung Chang, but spoke in Irish dialect." (Twain himself was no stranger to analogous gambits. In an early sketch called "A Visit to Niagara," the humor came from the fact that every "Indian" with whom the narrator tries to strike up a conversation turns out to speak Irish brogue. Twain, *Sketches, New and Old*, pp. 63–71.)

117. A chimney sweep is featured in one other work by Twain, "How the Chimney-Sweep Got the Ear of the Emperor," which appeared embedded in another story, "The Man With a Message for the Director-General" under the title "Two Little Tales," first published in 1901 in the *Century Magazine*. See Budd, *Collected Tales, Sketches, Speeches, & Essays, 1891–1910*, pp. 498–504. An example of vaudeville's Chimney Sweep/Baker routine was filmed in 1902 by the American Mutoscope and Biograph Company. It may be viewed online at the Library of Congress American Memory website (http://memory.loc.gov).

118. It is possible that two other minor features of *Is He Dead?* may also owe a debt to vaudeville: the choice of the first name "Daisy" for the widow and the choice of the surname "Bismarck" for Dutchy. "Daisy" jokes and characters named "Bismarck" figured frequently in vaudeville. Tony Pastor's vaudeville script "The 3 Confidence Men," for example, features a (male) character named Daisy who responds to the query, "You're a greenhorn?" with "No I ain't, I'm a Daisy. John Daisy of Daisy Farm" (Pastor Vaudeville Collection, in the Harry Ransom Humanities Research Center). And W. C. Robey's 1897 vaudeville script, *Li Hung Chang's Reception*, features Bismarck, "a German prince in disguise" (Twain wrote a note to accompany the crossed-out lines connecting Dutchy's last name to the name of the German chancellor Bismarck, noting that the reference would have constituted an anachronism).

119. Frank and Smith, *Twain's Letters*, vol. 6, pp. 387–89.

120. Daniel C. Gerould, "Introduction," *American Melodrama*, ed. Daniel C. Gerould (New York: Performing Arts Journal Publications, 1983), pp. 1, 10–11; Dion Boucicault, "The Poor of New York," in Gerould, *American Melodrama*, pp. 66–67; James L. Smith, *Melodrama* (London: Methuen, 1973), p. 19. It is worth noting that two of Twain's closest friends in the acting profession, William Gillette and Sir Henry Irving, both frequently performed in melodramas.

121. Peter Brooks, *The Melodramatic Imagination* (New Haven: Yale University Press, 1976), pp. 34–36; Gerould, "Introduction," *American Melodrama*, p. 9; Smith, *Melodrama*, p. 9.

122. Thomas Schirer notes that in amateur theatricals in Missouri when Twain was growing up, men often played women's parts. Schirer, *Twain and the Theatre*, p. 7. See also Elbert Russell Bowen, *Theatrical Entertainment in Rural Missouri Before the Civil War*, vol. 32, Uni-

versity of Missouri Studies (Columbia: University of Missouri Press, 1959). For more on these popular traditions, see Laurence Senelick, *The Changing Room: Sex, Drag and Theatre* (New York: Routledge, 2000). For discussions of the "dame" figure in pantomime, see D. Mayer, "The Sexuality of Pantomime," *Theatre Quarterly* (February–April 1974), pp. 55–54; and M. Eigner, "Imps, Dames and Principal Boys: Gender Confusion in the Nineteenth-Century Pantomime," *Browning Institute Studies* 17 (1989): 71–73; W. F. Sage, "Impersonators of Women," *Theatre* 5 (May 1889): 285; and Laurence Senelick, "Neil Burgess," *American National Biography*, vol. 3 (New York: Oxford University Press, 1999), pp. 941–43.

123. Robert C. Toll, *On With the Show: The First Century of Show Business in America* (New York: Oxford University Press, 1976), pp. 240, 242. For Twain's familiarity with the Christy Minstrels, see *Mark Twain in Eruption: Hitherto Unpublished Pages about Men and Events*, ed. Bernard DeVoto (New York: Harper & Brothers, 1940), p. 118.

124. Toll, *On With the Show*, p. 242.

125. *Clipper* quoted in Toll, *On With the Show*, p. 242. Leon quoted in Toll, *On With the Show*, p. 243. Male sopranos attired as elegant females performed in operas at Maguire's Opera House in San Francisco and, as Senelick notes, "the cross-dressed male soprano reigned supreme in the concert saloons of mining towns" (Senelick, *The Changing Room*, p. 298). Twain might well have seen men playing such roles in San Francisco or Virginia City, Nevada, in the 1860s.

126. John Bouvé Clapp and Edwin Francis Edgett, *Players of the Present, Part I* (New York: The Dunlap Society, 1899), pp. 46–47; and Lawrence Senelick, *The Changing Room*, p. 239.

127. Advertisement for Tony Pastor's Theatre, *New York Herald*, 24 December 1876, quoted in Geraldine Maschio, "Neil Burgess: Female Impersonation and the Image of the Victorian Matron," *Studies in Popular Culture* 8, no. 2 (1985): 52.

128. "Mr Clemmens, Dr Sir please accept the enclosed seats for this evening—and if I can amuse you in 'Vim' it will help pay the interest on the everlasting debt I owe you, for the great pleasure I have taken and still take in your works. Respectfully, your obedient servant, Neil Burgess." Burgess to Clemens, 28 October 1884, in the Mark Twain Papers. On the same day Twain wrote a letter from Hartford that said "My Dear Mr. Burgess: I am most heartily sorry, but my wife & I are booked for a social engagement, & thus are euchred out of the pleasure which you have so kindly offerd us. With my best thanks, I am Truly Yours Mark Twain." Clemens to Neil Burgess, 28 October 1884, photocopy in the Mark Twain Papers from Todd M. Axelrod; published in *Microfilm Edition of Mark Twain's Previously Unpublished Letters*, vol. 2.

129. The following review of Burgess's play appeared in the *Hartford Courant* (a paper Twain read regularly): "A fair audience witnessed the production of Neil Burgess's new play 'Vim' at the opera house last evening. The campaign has served largely to diminish the size of the audiences this season and last night proved no exception. Those who attended, however, were well repaid. From beginning to finish it was an occasion for laughter and amusement. Neil Burgess as Tryphena Puffy was as comical as ever, and John Palmer as Josiah Puffy was very good. The other parts were fairly well taken, and the bits were well received" (*Hartford Courant*, 28 October 1884, p. 2). In Notebook 28 (July 1888–May 1889), Twain wrote, "Neil Burgess has accepted a new play" (Browning, Frank, and Salamo, *Twain's*

Notebooks & Journals, vol. 3, p. 409). The new play was *The County Fair*, which opened at Proctor's Twenty-third Street Theatre on 5 March 1889.

130. Maschio, "Neil Burgess," pp. 52–53; Maschio continues that the actor's characteristic female impersonation was "a rural American version of Mrs. Malaprop . . . given to great pretensions in language and in etiquette despite her obviously humble background. . . . She was a larger than life character ripe for burlesque." W. F. Sage, "Impersonators of Women," *Theatre* 5 (May 1889): 285, quoted in Senelick, *The Changing Room*, p. 240. Odell described Burgess's act as follows: "A big man, without the slightest trace of good looks, he could, without difficulty, seem the woman he was playing, whether making a pie in the kitchen, giving a piece of her mind to an interfering interloper or starting a young couple on the way to matrimony. Nothing of the effect, somewhat unpleasing, that one associates with the young 'female impersonator' of vaudeville inhered in Burgess's wholesome, jolly characterizations." George C. D. Odell, *Annals of the New York Stage*, 15 vols. (New York: Columbia University Press, 1927–1949), vol. 14, p. 56.

131. Senelick, "Neil Burgess," p. 943.

132. Maschio, "Neil Burgess," p. 53.

133. A variation on Burgess's patented treadmill "eventually enabled Ben Hur to be successfully adapted for the stage." Senelick, "Neil Burgess," pp. 942, 943; for ubiquity of *County Fair* performances, see Senelick, *The Changing Room*, p. 239.

134. A lengthy profile of Neil Burgess as a member of the Players appears in John Bouvé Clapp and Edwin Francis Edgett, *Players of the Present, Part I* (New York: The Dunlap Society, 1899), pp. 46–47. It does not state the year that he joined the club. Laurence Hutton, a co-founder of the Players who was a close friend of Twain's, praised the "Widow Bedott" in his *Curiosities of the American Stage* (New York: Harper & Brothers, 1891), p. 44.

135. On the *Charley's Aunt* craze, see Jevan Brandon-Thomas, *Charley's Aunt's Father: A Life of Brandon Thomas* (London: Douglas Saunders with MacGibbon & Kee, 1955), p. 180. On the play's huge success, see Jeffrey H. Huberman, *Late Victorian Farce*, no. 40, Theater and Dramatic Studies (Ann Arbor: University of Michigan Research Press, 1986), p. 116.

136. Jevan Brandon-Thomas, *Charley's Aunt's Father*, pp. 188, 203, 206. Brandon Thomas's farce eventually would be translated into German, French, Japanese, Greek, Turkish, Scandinavian languages, Afrikaans, Gaelic, Zulu, and Esperanto. In one year it would play simultaneously in forty-eight different cities, in twenty-two different languages. Huberman, *Late Victorian Farce*, pp. 121, 232; "'Charley's Aunt' a Success. The New Farce from London Produced at the Standard Theatre," *New York Times*, 3 October 1893, p. 4. The reviewer went on to say, "Most impersonations of a woman by a man have an element, greater or smaller, of the repulsive . . . In Mr. Geradot's [sic] impersonation, this element is altogether lacking. . . ." Actor Etienne Girardot played Lord Fancourt Babberly and "Babbs," his impersonation of Charley's Aunt, in the play.

137. Twain lived at the Players club from late September 1893 until March 1894.

138. The *New York Times* reported that the audience at the play "fairly howled with laughter" throughout the production at Girardot's portrayal of Charley's Aunt (3 October 1893, p. 4). The performance was the young English actor's American debut. Odell recalls in his entry on *Charley's Aunt* in his *Annals of the New York Stage* for 1893 that "Etienne Girardot made a tremendous hit as the undergraduate disguised as the aunt from Brazil; I

do not see how the much-vaunted London creator of the part, W. S. Penley, could have been funnier or more plausible in the woman's dress he was forced to wear . . . I met him many times, in these years, at The Players, a club we both loved and often frequented." Odell, *Annals of the New York Stage*, vol. 15, p. 599.

139. The Savage Club, which elected Twain an honorary member in 1897, was Brandon Thomas's favorite club (he had been a member since 1883). Jevan Brandon-Thomas, *Charley's Aunt's Father*, p. 86. Although the volume misdates Twain's election to honorary membership as 1899, see *The Savage Club: A Medley of History, Anecdote and Reminiscence by Aaron Watson, with a Chapter by Mark Twain* (London: T. Fisher Unwin, 1907), pp. 131–35, for Twain's comments on the club; Brandon Thomas's active participation is noted on p. 291, and he is pictured in the sketch of club members. Twain frequently spent time at the club during sojourns in London in the 1890s. Brandon Thomas was also close to the actor Sir Henry Irving, who was such a good friend of Twain's that he gave him a "perpetual free ticket" to his theatres. In November 1893, Twain wrote a friend with a request that he "Please look in the wardrobe-drawer next to the washbowl in Mrs. Clemens's bathroom & find my perpetual free-ticket to Irving's theatres. It is oval, is made of bone stained red, & looks something like this [here Twain drew a picture of it]." Clemens to Franklin G. Whitmore, 14 November 1893, in the Mark Twain House, Hartford, Conn.; published in *Microfilm Edition of Mark Twain's Previously Unpublished Letters*, vol. 4. Twain socialized with Irving in December 1893, the season of *Charley's Aunt*'s triumph in New York. See Clemens to Olivia Langdon Clemens, 18 November 1893, in Wecter, *Love Letters*, pp. 278–79. See Clemens to Olivia Langdon Clemens, 8 December 1893, in the Mark Twain Papers; also available in *Microfilm Edition of Mark Twain's Manuscript Letters Now in the Mark Twain Papers*, vol. 7. See Clemens to Joseph H. Twichell, 20 November 1893, in the Beinecke Rare Book and Manuscript Library, Yale University; published in *Microfilm Edition of Mark Twain's Previously Unpublished Letters*, vol. 4. They might well have discussed the play because, in addition to being friends with the playwright, Irving was friends with the English actor Percy Lyndal, who was then playing Jack Chesney, one of the leading roles. (Lyndal had accompanied Irving during his tour to the United States in 1883–1884; Twain entertained Irving at his Hartford home during that tour.)

140. Brandon Thomas, *Charley's Aunt: A Play in Three Acts* [1892] (copyright 1933 by Jevan Roderick Brandon-Thomas and William Deane Barnes-Brand; New York: Samuel French, 1935), p. 89.

141. Senelick, *The Changing Room*, p. 241.

142. Huberman, *Late Victorian Farce*, p. 121.

143. Quoted in Jevan Brandon-Thomas, *Charley's Aunt's Father*, p. 155.

144. Quoted in Huberman, *Late Victorian Farce*, p. 124.

145. Paine, *Biography*, vol. 2, pp. 994–95; Howard G. Baetzhold, *Mark Twain and John Bull: The British Connection* (Bloomington: Indiana University Press, 1970), p. 197; Barbara Belford, *Bram Stoker* (New York: Alfred A. Knopf, 1996), pp. 164–65, 282–83.

146. "Feb. 12. From letter to Bram Stoker: If he is willing, his commission for acting as agent for my plays, to 15% of the profits accruing to me, all over the world, & *he* to pay the commissions of all of his sub-agents out of his 15%." Notebook 40, typescript p. 12, in the

Mark Twain Papers; also available in *Microfilm Edition of Mark Twain's Literary Manuscripts Available in the Mark Twain Papers*, vol. 33.

147. Twain wrote Rogers that he was putting "the finishing touches" on *Is He Dead?* in a letter dated February 5–6. By March 7, Stoker had already given the play a first reading and sent Twain his response.

148. Harry Ludlum, *A Biography of Dracula: The Life Story of Bram Stoker* (London: The Fireside Press/W. Foulsham, 1962), pp. 116–17; Bram Stoker, *Personal Reminiscences of Henry Irving*, 2 vols. (New York: Macmillan, 1906), vol. 2, pp. 297–303; Belford, *Bram Stoker*, pp. 278–79.

149. Stoker, *Personal Reminiscences of Henry Irving*, vol. 2, pp. 301, 302. The loss was particularly severe since Irving's productions were known for being "magnificent syntheses of spectacular settings and costumes, effective music, and impressive acting." Glenn Hughes, *A History of the American Theatre, 1700–1950* (New York: Samuel French, 1951), p. 255. The "spectacular settings and costumes" were now completely gone.

150. Ludlam, *Biography of Dracula*, pp. 116–17; Stoker, *Personal Reminiscences of Henry Irving*, vol. 2, p. 325–26.

151. The context for this statement is as follows: "Bram Stoker is willing to be my dramatic agent in England and maybe in America; and I asked him because I was ashamed to ask you to potter with it. He has not said he would act for America, and I hope he will decline; for if *you* don't mind, I would rather have you for dramatic agent than any other expert in the business, I don't care where he hails from. [¶]On a first reading he doesn't much believe in my play, but says he is going to examine it more closely" (Clemens to Rogers, 7 March 1898, Leary, *Correspondence with Rogers*, pp. 323–24).

152. "Bram Stoker has sent you my so-called play. Thinks it is good ~~enough~~ for America, possibly—not for England. *I* think that if it were put into the hands of a professional playwright it might perhaps be made a playing piece. An American one, I mean. Frohman, of the Lyceum Theatre, used to have such a man. There are others, but I don't know them" (Clemens to Rogers, 15 March 1898, Leary, *Correspondence with Rogers*, p. 326).

153. Clemens to Rogers, 15 March 1898, Leary, *Correspondence with Rogers*, p. 326.

154. Things got only worse. Within the year, depressed by the loss of all scenery and props he needed to put on plays and weakened by pneumonia and pleurisy, Irving would sell the Lyceum to a syndicate without consulting Stoker. The fire in February had been the beginning of the end. Stoker and Twain remained friends and saw each other occasionally in later years.

155. Clemens to Rogers, 15 March 1898, Leary, *Correspondence with Rogers*, p. 326. On April 21, Twain wrote Rogers that "Charles Frohman (Savoy Hotel, London) wants to see my play. I have written him that he'd better apply to you, as you have the only copy that anybody can read. I told him you wrote that you were going to submit it to the Frohmans." Clemens to Rogers, 21 April 1898, Leary, *Correspondence with Rogers*, p. 343. Charles Frohman and his brother Daniel exerted enormous control over the theatre. Charles Frohman was "one of the all-powerful six men who controlled" the theatrical syndicate that had been formed by the 1870s for "controlling the booking, managing, and housing of touring companies throughout the country" (Goldman, "Mark Twain as a Playwright," p. 115). Frohman's response to *Is He Dead?* is unknown.

156. Clemens to Rogers, 26 July 1898, Leary, *Correspondence with Rogers*, p. 353.

157. Alf Hayman to C. C. Rice, 27 February 1899, in Alderman Library, University of Virginia.

158. Klaw and Erlanger to Alf Hayman, 2 February 1899, in Alderman Library, University of Virginia. Neither Klaw and Erlanger nor Twain himself seems to have pursued revising the play. But, three years later, in 1902, Klaw and Erlanger contracted with him to produce a musical version of *Huckleberry Finn*. Twain had little to do with the musical, which was written by a Southern playwright named Lee Arthur and bore more resemblance to *Tom Sawyer* than to *Huckleberry Finn*. See Michael Patrick Hearn, "Introduction," *The Annotated Huckleberry Finn* (New York: W. W. Norton, 2001), pp. cx–cxi; and Brooks McNamara, "*Huckleberry Finn* on Stage: A Mark Twain Letter in the Shubert Archive," *The Passing Show* (Fall 1991), p. 2.

159. Clemens to Rogers, 18 April 1899, Leary, *Correspondence with Rogers*, p. 393.

160. Huberman, *Late Victorian Farce*, p. 129.

161. Ibid.

162. Ibid., pp. 130–31.

163. Klaw and Erlanger to Alf Hayman, 2 February 1899, in Alderman Library, University of Virginia.

164. Huberman, *Late Victorian Farce*, p. 134.

165. Twain wrote Bettina Wirth: "I sent the play to my business friend in New York & said I would translate it if it was likely to make a success there. The response was not sufficiently encouraging—war-plays are all the go there, these days . . . Sincerely Yours, S L Clemens." Clemens to Mrs. [Bettina] Wirth, 19 June 1898, in the Mark Twain House, Hartford, Conn.; published in *Microfilm Edition of Mark Twain's Previously Unpublished Letters*, vol. 5. The "war-plays" comment is supported in part by a facsimile of a page of theatre advertisements from "a New York newspaper" of 7 May 1898 that Twain reprints in his essay "About Play-Acting" that appeared in New York's *Forum* in October 1898 and was later reprinted in his *Man that Corrupted Hadleyburg* (p. 237). The page includes notices of performances of what might be considered "war plays." These include ads for "Edison's Wonderful War-Scope" at Pastor's theatre; "The Man-o'-War's Man" at the Fourteenth Street Theatre; "Battles of Our Nation" at the Academy of Music; and "War Bubbles" followed by "An Original Patriotic Extravaganza" at the Olympic Music Hall.

166. Howells to Clemens, 2 August 1898, Smith and Gibson, *Twain-Howells Letters*, p. 673.

167. Huberman, *Late Victorian Farce*, p. 132. Huberman notes that "in view of the consistent failure of farces produced in London in the last seven years of the decade, entrepreneurial enthusiasm for the form began to wane. From a post-*Charley's Aunt* high of twenty-five farces produced in 1895, the number fell to sixteen in 1896, fourteen in 1897, twelve in 1898, and finally eleven in 1899. These figures do show, however, that a significant number of managers were still speculating on the chance that they might find another hit like *Charley's Aunt*. . . . The more successful speculators, however, were investing in new forms of drama that began to catch the public fancy in these years—dramatic forms that were largely anathema to the nature of farce" (p. 122). Huberman notes that some of the forms that replaced farce in popularity were comedies of manners (such as those by Wilde) and "thesis" comedies (such as those by Shaw).

168. The only play Twain wrote after *Is He Dead?* was *The Death Wafer*, an eminently forgettable

and dull dramatization of his story "The Death Disk." It was written in 1900, runs 58 pages in manuscript, and was performed informally at the Carnegie Lyceum. He did not try to get it produced. (The manuscript is in the Mark Twain Papers.)

169. Bernard DeVoto, *Mark Twain at Work* (Cambridge: Harvard University Press, 1942), pp. 115–16; Forrest Robinson, "A Brief Biography," in *Historical Guide to Mark Twain*, ed. Shelley Fisher Fishkin (New York: Oxford University Press, 2002), p. 47; see also William. R. Macnaughton, *Mark Twain's Last Years as a Writer* (Columbia: University of Missouri Press, 1979); Hamlin Hill, *Mark Twain. God's Fool* (New York: Harper & Row, 1973); and Peter Messent, *The Short Works of Mark Twain: A Critical Study* (Philadelphia: University of Pennsylvania Press, 2001).

170. Robinson, "Brief Biography," p. 26.

171. Andrew Hoffman, *Inventing Mark Twain: The Lives of Samuel Langhorne Clemens* (New York: William Morrow, 1997), p. 424.

172. For a lucid consideration of the issue of imposture and identity in Twain's work, see Gillman, *Dark Twins*.

173. See Shelley Fisher Fishkin, "Mark Twain and Women," in *The Cambridge Companion to Mark Twain*, ed. Forrest Robinson (New York: Cambridge University Press, 1995), pp. 52–73. See also Peter Stoneley, *Mark Twain and the Feminine Aesthetic* (Cambridge: Cambridge University Press, 1992); Laura Skandera-Trombley, *Mark Twain in the Company of Women* (Philadelphia: University of Pennsylvania Press, 1994); and Gregg Camfield, *Sentimental Twain: Samuel Clemens in the Maze of Moral Philosophy* (Philadelphia: University of Pennsylvania Press, 1994). Joyce Warren charged in 1984 that Twain's "novels show us humorous old ladies and silly little girls, but there is no woman of any substance. . . . For the most part, Twain is simply not interested in the female characters in his works." Joyce W. Warren, "Old Ladies and Little Girls," *The American Narcissus: Individualism and Women in Nineteenth-Century American Fiction* (New Brunswick, N.J.: Rutgers University Press, 1984), pp. 149–50; quote from p. 150. For similar arguments see Judith Fryer, *The Faces of Eve: Women in the Nineteenth Century American Novel* (New York: Oxford University Press, 1976) and Wilma Garcia, *Mothers and Others: Myths of the Female in the Works of Melville, Twain and Hemingway* (New York: Peter Lang, 1984).

174. See Fishkin, "Mark Twain and Women," for this argument. For additional insights on this topic, see Susan Harris, "Mark Twain and Gender," in Fishkin, *A Historical Guide to Mark Twain*.

175. See Senelick, *The Changing Room*; Judith Butler, *Gender Trouble: Feminism and the Subversion of Identity* (New York: Routledge, 1990), pp. 137–39; and Marjorie B. Garber, *Vested Interests: Cross-dressing and Cultural Anxiety* (New York: Routledge, 1992).

176. Senelick, *The Changing Room*, p. 3. Senelick writes that "the transvestite in the theatre does not confute or elude categories; it creates new ones . . ." (p. 11).

177. Judith Butler, for example, clarifies and modifies aspects of positions on this topic that readers read into her earlier book, *Gender Trouble*, in her later book, *Bodies that Matter: On the Discursive Limits of "Sex"* (New York: Routledge, 1993), pp. 124–37. See also Elaine Showalter, "Critical Cross-Dressing: Male Feminists and the Woman of the Year," in *Raritan Reading*, ed. Richard Poirier (New Brunswick, N.J.: Rutgers University Press, 1990), pp. 369–70. In an article entitled "Drag=Blackface" published in the *Chicago-Kent Law*

Review in 2000 (no. 75: 669–70), Kelly Kleiman claims that drag is always offensive to women, arguing "that a whole range of activities from vaudeville 'illusionists' to the pantomime dame, from *Doubtfire* to *La Cage Aux Folles*, from cross-dresser balls in Harlem to Hasty Pudding theatricals at Harvard, represent institutionalized male hostility to women on a spectrum running from prescription of desired behavior to simple ridicule. These performances may be glamorous or comic, presented by gay men or straight men. Nonetheless, all of them represent a continuing insult to women, as is apparent from the parallels between these performances and those of white performers of blackface minstrelsy."

ACKNOWLEDGMENTS

The offices of the Mark Twain Papers at The Bancroft Library of the University of California at Berkeley are filled with treasures. There are treasures lurking in the file cabinets, to be sure, but there are also treasures hunched over the desks. I owe a great debt to General Editor Robert H. Hirst, and to Victor Fischer, Michael Frank, Lin Salamo, Anh Bui, and Harriet Elinor Smith, the dedicated band of editors there, who, under Bob Hirst's guidance, established the text of *Is He Dead?* in this volume and so generously shared their time and expertise with me. I'd also like to thank Neda Salem, administrative assistant at the Mark Twain Papers, for her help in this project.

My editor at the University of California Press, Laura Cerruti, was a joy to work with: a fount of energy, inspiration, and good ideas. My agent, Sam Stoloff, believed in this project from the start and helped make it happen every step of the way. I am grateful to the scholars who helped me learn what I needed to know to write this book, whether the subject was the history of cross-dressing on stage, or Millet's place in the Boston art world, or vaudeville dialect, or melodrama, or Japanese adaptations of Twain's works. These include Tish Burnham, Gregg Camfield, Charlotte Canning, Wanda Corn, Tsuyoshi Ishihara, Gavin Jones, Stephen Orgel, R. W. Shoch, John A. Stokes, and Bryan Wolf.

The staff of the Theatre Arts collections at both the Harry Ransom Humanities Research Center at the University of Texas at Austin and at Harvard University were very helpful, as were the staffs of the Fine Arts Library and Perry-Castañeda Library at the University of Texas and Stanford University's Green Library. Thanks especially to Pat Fox, Nicolette Schneider, and John Kirkpatrick at the Harry Ransom Humanities Research Center and to Annette Fern at Harvard. I am also grateful to the following archives and collectors for increasing the scope of the Mark Twain Papers by providing The Bancroft Library with photocopies of original letters by Samuel L. Clemens: Alderman Library, University of Virginia, Charlottesville; Todd M. Axelrod, Las Vegas, Nevada; Beinecke Rare Book and Manuscript Library, Yale University, New Haven, Conn.; Mark Twain House, Hartford, Conn.; Pierpont Morgan Library, New York; and Rare Book and Special Collections Library, University of Illinois, Urbana. Tracy Wuster was the most resourceful and enterprising research assistant on the planet. Ashlee Brown was a pro at tracking down recondite articles. Kathleen MacDougall was a careful and conscientious copyeditor. A grant from the University of Texas at Austin helped support my research. Janice Bradley, Suzanne Colwell, and Cynthia Frese of the American Studies Department at the University of Texas made it possible for me to do this research and writing while chairing a department.

David Bradley, Chiyuma Elliott, Cary Franklin, Hal Holbrook, Calvin and Maria Johnson, David Krasner, Jeffrey Meikle, Hilton Obenzinger, Margaret Osborne, Arnold Rampersad, and Lillian Robinson offered encouragement and good advice. I want to thank Bob Boyett, Ken Burrows, Richard Watson, Dan Werner, and Robert Youdelman for working with me to make *Is He Dead?* into a play that might play some day.

I owe a great debt to my son Bobby, an award-winning playwright who helped me understand some of the challenges Twain faced in this role; to my son Joey, that rarest of creatures: a graduate student who is both a superb writer and a remarkable editor; and to my stepmother, Carol Fisher, who shared my excitement and helped make it all more fun.

But my greatest thanks are due to my husband, Jim Fishkin, who generously shared his wife with that other man in her life, the guy who's been his rival for her attention for their entire marriage: Mark Twain.

DESIGNER Nicole Hayward   ILLUSTRATOR Barry Moser
TEXT 10.5/13 Filosofia   DISPLAY Filosophia Unicase and Akzidenz Grotesk
COMPOSITOR Integrated Composition Systems, Inc.   PRINTER AND BINDER Edwards Brothers